TARGETED
READING
INTERVENTIONS

FOR THE COMMON CORE

CLASSROOM-TESTED LESSONS THAT HELP
STRUGGLING STUDENTS MEET THE RIGORS OF THE STANDARDS

Diana Sisson & Betsy Sisson

■ SCHOLASTIC

New York • Toronto • London • Auckland • Sydney
Mexico City • New Delhi • Hong Kong • Buenos Aires

DEDICATION

*To our parents, Lin and Ruth Sisson, who instilled within us
a love of learning and a lifelong commitment to education*

Cover Designer: Jorge J. Namerow
Interior Designer: Sarah Morrow
Development Editor: Joanna Davis-Swing
Editor: Sarah Glasscock
Copy Editor: David Klein

Copyright © 2014 by Diana Sisson and Betsy Sisson
All rights reserved. Published by Scholastic Inc.
Printed in the U.S.A.
ISBN: 978-0-545-65780-8

2 3 4 5 6 7 8 9 10 40 22 21 20 19 18 17 16

CONTENTS

Introduction

Two of the most significant events in the field of education are coalescing in classrooms around the country: Common Core State Standards (CCSS, 2010) and Response to Intervention (RtI). The writers who drafted the CCSS emphasize that they designed the standards to address the question of "what" rather than "how." While this approach allows for flexibility in the implementation of the standards, it also leaves many unanswered questions about how to proceed in ways that adhere to the best practices in literacy. Of concern are the estimated one in three students who struggle to learn to read (Greenwood, Kamps, Terry, & Linebarger, 2007). RtI offers the structured, prescriptive format needed to address the standards for these students.

Enacted in 2006, RtI is the culmination of over three decades of federal involvement in special education services. It has two overarching goals: (1) to identify at-risk students and provide intensive intervention prior to the development of severe deficits and disability identification, and (2) to identify students with learning disabilities who are chronically unresponsive to standardized forms of instruction and, instead, necessitate individualized, data-based instruction (Fuchs, Fuchs, & Vaughn, 2008).

One of the primary attributes of the RtI model is the implementation of a multi-tiered approach to student support and intervention (Barnes & Harlacher, 2008; Mellard & Johnson, 2008). Most school systems adhere to three specialized tiers. Tier I centers on core instruction implemented in the classroom. Tier II, for those who don't respond to core instruction, provides targeted interventions in small groups of approximately four to six students, once or twice a week. Students who continue to struggle transition to the intensive interventions of Tier III and work three to five times a week in prescriptive groups of no more than three students.

This text can be used at any of these three tiers, but it is specifically designed for students who struggle at Tier II, or even Tier III. To address the needs of these students, we have carefully and purposefully crafted activities that are:

- Research-based
- Aligned to standards
- Proactive and preventive
- Systematic and explicit
- Formatted for small groups of no more than six students

Understanding the importance of academic interventions, we wrote this book to offer insights into what the CCSS standards are, why they are important, and how they can easily be implemented in grades 4 and up. What do we do with students who cannot master these standards? How do we provide varied instructional supports that are essential for students' success? What approaches will be the most effective for accomplishing these challenges? This book provides the bridge to interventions grounded in clear pedagogical theory and research.

We look at instruction through three distinct lenses. First, we base our work in the developmental psychology theories of Vygotsky, especially focusing on the Zone of Proximal Development (ZPD). ZPD refers to the difference between what a child can achieve independently and what he or she can achieve through guidance and support (Vygotsky, 1962, 1978). We follow this principle by starting instruction at the student's current skill level, providing scaffolded support, and guiding the development of skills that the student will eventually use independently.

Second, we use Bloom's Taxonomy to frame students' cognitive development (Bloom, 1956). Encompassing six levels (knowledge, comprehension, application, analysis, synthesis, and evaluation) of intellectual processing, Bloom's premise is that learners cannot progress to the next level before mastering the previous one. Because of his influence in our approach with struggling readers, we focus on providing systematic activities that build off one another so struggling students can steadily increase their skills through a carefully planned cognitive progression.

Third, the recent work of Heacox in differentiation and her emphasis on the importance of KUDOs has been profoundly important in our focus on structured, scaffolded exposure to concepts and skills (Heacox, 2009). KUDOs is an acronym for what we need students to accomplish in three specific areas.

- **K**now (the definitions, facts, and so on, that students memorize for basic recall)

- **U**nderstand (the "big ideas" that students take away from instruction)

- **DO** (the skills and tasks that students are expected to perform independently)

This template allows teachers to scaffold student learning through a systematic approach designed to chunk learning into meaningful parts as students gradually transition to independence. Stemming from Bloom's Taxonomy, KUDOs offers an instructional tool that also helps us critically analyze the essence of the content we want students to master as we reflect on key knowledge that they must acquire, the essential understanding underlying the content, and what specific goals we envision for students.

With more than 30 years of combined experience in the field working with students at every grade level, we believe that, in addition to educational theory, there are certain principles that should guide instructional practice as well. These principles have the power to affect student learning, and more significantly, to ultimately influence performance outcomes. If you look at these principles, or drivers for change, as a sequence of instructional planning, they provide a blueprint for effective interventions.

Principles to Guide Instructional Practice

1. **Focus on the essence of the content.** What exactly are we expecting from our students? At the very core of our instructional goals, what do we want students to be able to do independently? Once you answer those questions, you will have an incisive focus on which to base all of your work.

2. **Link content to personal connections.** Struggling students often feel disengaged from content and fail to see its relevance to their own lives. Add to that their frustration with making meaning from text, and you have a prescription for failure before you begin. To combat that, look for ways to connect the content to students' own experiences. Show them the relevance of the text and its value to them. Make the content important to their daily lives.

3. **Use short pieces of text.** Lengthy pieces of text can be overwhelming to struggling readers. Before you can begin to discuss content and demonstrate a concept, students may have shut down their own learning. How can they understand what you want to teach them if they are

still trying to construct meaning from the words on the page? To remove that barrier, teach from brief texts that appear accessible and manageable to those students.

4. **Chunk the process.** As with the texts themselves, content can appear protracted and difficult to navigate. As you plan how to deliver instruction, think about what you expect learners to do. How can you break that down into pieces where students can focus on only one component? Once you do that, you can show students the sequence of the text in simple steps—rather than as one inexplicable entity.

5. **Engage the senses.** The more ways we engage students' thinking, the greater their ability to practice and retain the content. Can they see it? Can they talk about it with others, both through listening and sharing their own thoughts? Can they complete a performance task in which they create something to demonstrate their understanding? Challenge yourself to design as many formats as possible for repeated exposure. Each instance allows the learning to deepen.

6. **Develop visual representations of content.** Closely linked to engaging the senses, this instructional driver emphasizes illustrations, charts, and graphics that provide explicit explanation of the content. For students who perceive reading as a mysterious, abstract process, visual representations can often furnish the missing link between the expectations we hold for content learning and students' current level of understanding.

7. **Ensure opportunities for success.** What defines a struggling reader? They struggle with text . . . again and again and again. In many cases, this constant sense of failure becomes a self-fulfilling prophecy: *Why bother trying? I am only going to fail.* If this is the mind-set of a student, then nothing you do is going to help until his or her experiences change. How do you do that? You construct opportunities for that student to blossom. Give your students initial activities in which you know they will feel successful, such as those that link the content to their personal lives. It may be through a particularly easy text that you know they can read independently. It may even be through an activity you know they really like. It doesn't matter what you choose. The point is to make certain students succeed.

8. **Incorporate guided practice.** How do basketball players get better? They practice with a coach who observes them in action, shows them how to improve, and steers them in the right direction. How is that different for struggling readers? It isn't. Guided practice is essential if you are going to track what students understand and what they don't, provide ongoing support, and give them the confidence they need to master the content.

9. **Integrate collaborative activities.** An overriding psychological factor that commonly impedes struggling readers is a sense of isolation. They commonly view reading as a solitary task that they must complete alone and unaided. To dispel this mind-set, you should design collaborative activities in which struggling readers work and learn with others.

10. **Supply layered feedback.** Layered feedback, encompassing three levels of instructional support, is absolutely critical for struggling readers. One, when students perform an academic task successfully, you should summarize which skills and thinking they employed in an explicit, clear recap to ensure that they are cognizant of how they achieved success as well as how to replicate that success in other contexts. Two, when students are grappling with a task, you should engage them in a conversation to help them trace their thinking back to the point where their understanding broke down. Determining where the disconnect between their knowledge and the content happened allows students to see that they did have partial success. Also, if you do

not find the disconnect, you cannot help students improve because you do not know where their understanding fractured. Three, if students fail at a particular task, you need to talk them through the process. Show them how to achieve success in small, manageable steps.

How to Use This Book

We have interwoven these instructional drivers throughout the book, providing a detailed explanation of each of the College and Career Readiness Anchor Standards for Reading with interventions in both literature and informational text.

Each chapter of this book highlights one anchor standard. We also recommend the KUDOs necessary for promoting powerful instruction for that standard. Then we analyze the standard's pedagogical purpose and rationale for inclusion in high-quality instruction and follow that with the transitional steps for mastery that illustrate how students progress throughout the grades with an increasingly more complex and sophisticated skill set.

Although this text centers on the work of students in grades 4 and up, we have included transitional steps to grade twelve to demonstrate the continuum of learning students must acquire throughout their academic career and, equally, to emphasize how important the work you do is—not just to the learning of students today, but also as a foundation for the learning these students must accomplish tomorrow.

Each activity in a chapter includes the underlying principles for how these interventions provide prescriptive support for the needs of struggling students, along with a list of any materials you'll need to carry out these engaging, hands-on interventions. The activities align to the Common Core State Standards; each chapter begins with grade 4 and progresses to secondary expectations. Instructionally, you can implement the activities that correspond to the grade-level expectations of your students, or you can move back to previous activities if you feel they lack foundational skills from prior grades. As you begin to implement these interventions in your classroom, use the focus questions at the bottom of each activity to scaffold students' thinking and understanding of the content. You can decide how many focus questions to ask; they are designed to help you structure your students' interactions with the text and/or activity. Note that we often provide variations of the same question to help expand students' experience with these kinds of questions.

A Note About Selecting Texts: For each activity that requires a text, we offer general suggestions for selecting a suitable text, but we rarely recommend a specific title. We have made this decision thoughtfully and intentionally for the following reasons.

First, we don't want our readers to infer that a suggested text is the "best" possible resource. You shouldn't feel compelled to purchase or locate a text in the belief that the activity cannot be done without that specific text. In actuality, you can utilize texts you already have access to. You should be able to implement these activities immediately without having to locate additional resources.

Second, we have designed these activities to be flexible, fluid, and applicable to a range of genres, topics, reading levels, and grades. Suggesting a specific title would negate this aim and limit the text's appropriateness for students you target for intervention. A title we suggest may be too difficult for students in your group. Similarly, a title we recommend may not be challenging enough for your students. Furthermore, if your students lack foundational skills, it is good instructional practice to discover where the gap exists in their understanding and scaffold from that entry point—rather than simply beginning at their current grade-level placement.

Third, our hope is that this book will empower you to think about how you can use your resources in varied ways to provide effective, prescriptive instruction. What's more, we believe that students should be cognizant that books—be they fiction or nonfiction—can be viewed through multiple lenses. Rather than searching for a new text for every standard, consider that a single text can speak to numerous standards. For example, we often use the fairy tale, "Cinderella," for initial discussions about text as it is a universal narrative told in over 300 cultures and it allows student to focus on the literacy skills we are building and not on comprehending a new story. As we show below, you can use this one story as an exemplar text to teach nearly all the Common Core State Standards.

Standard 1 (Reading for Details): *At what time must Cinderella return from the ball? Why do you believe that Cinderella suddenly reveals herself to the prince when he is in her home with her missing shoe? Use details from the text to support your answer.*

Standard 2 (Theme/Summarization): *What is the theme of this story? Use details from the text to support your answer. What happens in this story? Be sure to include all of the important events.*

Standard 3 (Narrative Elements): *Why do you think Cinderella's stepmother treats Cinderella the way she does? Use details from the text to explain your answer.*

Standard 4 (Vocabulary): *The word "ball" has multiple meanings. How is it used in this text? Use details to explain your answer.*

Standard 5 (Text Structure): *What is the text structure of this story? How do you know? How would the story change if it were a different text structure? Would it change your understanding of the story?*

Standard 6 (Point of View/Author's Purpose): *From what point of view is the story related? How would the story change if it were related through the point of view of Cinderella's stepsisters? For what purpose do you think that this story was originally told? Be sure to use details from the story to explain your thinking.*

Standard 7 (Diverse Text Formats and Media): Read the story. Then watch a video of it. *How are the story and the video alike? How are they different? Use specific examples to explain your answers.*

Standard 8 (Evaluate Arguments in a Text): Not applicable to literature

Standard 9 (Comparing and Contrasting Multiple Texts): Read two different versions of "Cinderella." *Does the theme of the story change between the two versions of the story? Use details from both texts to explain your answer.*

Standard 10 (Variety of Genres and Levels of Text Complexity): Use "Cinderella" as a scaffold to guide students in reading a more complex text.

That's how easy it is to use one text for multiple standards. Not only will concentrating on one text make your instructional planning easier, but it will also demonstrate to students how to read a text more deeply and with more consideration. So, please, utilize these activities to offer prescriptive interventions that best meet the needs of your students.

In the Appendix, you'll find an introduction to the Common Core State Reading Standards (CCR1–10) and KUDOs as well as a list of additional resources. All of these materials support the goals of this text as well as the work that you do.

* * *

The landscape of the American classroom is changing. We cannot simply react; we must actively engage in reform and seek out ways to redesign our instructional practice—especially with our most vulnerable students. We hope this book will help you along your way.

Targeted Reading Interventions for the Common Core © 2014 by Diana Sisson & Betsy Sisson, Scholastic Teaching Resources

CHAPTER 1

Reading for Details Using Both Literal and Inferential Understanding

Read closely to determine what the text says explicitly and to make logical inferences from it; cite specific textual evidence when writing or speaking to support conclusions drawn from the text (CCSS, p. 10).

What students need to . . .

KNOW

- Logical inferences
- Textual evidence
- Conclusions

UNDERSTAND

- Conclusions are drawn by combining a reader's prior knowledge with information from the text.
- Conclusions must be drawn from relevant details from the text.
- Having support for a conclusion is an important aspect of drawing a conclusion.

DO

- Read text closely.
- Make logical inferences.
- Cite specific textual evidence.
- Support conclusions drawn from text.

Pedagogical Foundations

As a building block in developing reading comprehension skills, CCR1 falls within the first cluster of standards, Key Ideas and Details. Before students can determine craft and structure, integrate knowledge and ideas from text, or read and comprehend complex literary and informational text, they must first understand the explicit message of selected texts and be able to draw conclusions about what they read. As such, it is imperative that teachers focus on literal comprehension to ensure that students take the first step to independent reading (Basaraba, Yovanoff, Alonzo, & Tindal, 2013; Herber, 1970; Kintsch & Rawson, 2005; Nation, 2005; Perfetti, Marron, & Foltz, 1996). Following an explicit understanding of key details and the author's message, students must learn to think deductively and link their conclusions to evidentiary support.

●●●●●●●●●●●

Transitional Steps for Student Mastery

Beginning in kindergarten, students should be able to answer questions about key details in a text and transition to specific inquiries regarding who, what, when, where, why, and how by the end of second grade. While students in grade three provide explicit support for their responses, grade four marks the first year that inferential thinking appears as a benchmark for reading achievement. This focus intensifies in grade seven when students must cite multiple pieces of textual evidence to support their thinking, and then in grade eight when students must analyze which of the selected evidence most strongly supports their analysis of both the explicit text message and their inferential reasoning. By grade eleven, students must add to their accumulated skills the ability to determine where selected texts leave matters uncertain.

Tied to Texts

Inferential thinking is a complex task for any student. For a struggling reader already encumbered with making meaning from text and grappling with words at a literal comprehension level, trying to think inferentially can be self-defeating. As with all new skills, and especially with one as problematic as inferring, we start by giving students a successful experience with using the skill in their own lives.

Directions

Lead a discussion on drawing conclusions and the importance of supporting rational conclusions with details—both in life and in text. Ask students to name two adjectives that best describe themselves. Then, instruct them to identify facts about themselves that make these adjectives realistically match their personalities. Next, pair students. Invite them to "introduce" themselves to their partners, sharing the words and the supporting facts they have chosen for themselves.

Focus Questions

1. How would you describe yourself?

2. Upon which facts do you base that description?

Extension Activity

* After students have had sufficient time to "get to know" each other, ask volunteers to introduce their partners to the class, using the adjectives and facts their partner provided.

Three Steps to Mastering Inferential Reasoning

Students struggle with inferential thinking for a variety of reasons. Sometimes they are so text-bound that they confine their thoughts to the exact words in the passage and process only literal information. Others rely so heavily on their personal experiences that they overlook the facts in the passage that point to logical conclusions. Some readers are hesitant to venture an interpretation of a text for fear of being wrong. To counteract these problems, we offer students the simple formula at the right.

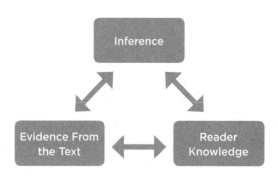

Several preliminary activities can build foundational understanding of the skills necessary to infer.

- **Mood ID:** One fun activity is to model exaggerated body language and facial expressions (e.g., bored, sad, happy, angry) and ask students to identify the mood they see and the supporting details that led them to this conclusion. This activity requires no written text and can quickly help students develop confidence.

- **What's So Funny?:** Another initial activity to encourage students to make inferences involves showing them cartoons with written captions. To understand what makes these cartoons humorous, the reader must be able to infer the meaning of the text. The cartoons provide a simple context for inferring, a child-friendly format to help students understand the relevance of the skill and, of course, an opportunity to practice the skill.

Materials

- Age-appropriate cartoons (optional)

Directions

Inferential skills are often hard to grasp for struggling readers. Provide them with support using the following process:

Step 1: Begin by simply asking students questions about a text and guiding them in identifying evidence from the text to support their answers.

Step 2: After students have demonstrated the ability to make an inference and provide support for it, ask them to share their thoughts about the evidence they found—how they located it and how it helped them make an inference.

Step 3: Again, after they have had multiple successful experiences at this level, transition to modeling and guiding students through the process of using explicit details from the text, along with their own thoughts and background knowledge, to draw reasonable conclusions.

Step 4: If students fail to use inferential reasoning in answering a question, go back to Step 1 to determine where the disconnect is originating and provide a self-correcting strategy they can use independently.

Focus Questions

1. What evidence from the text supports your answer? How do you know?

2. What do you know about the evidence from the text? Think about what you have read, heard, or experienced about this topic.

3. What inference can you make when you think about what the text says and what you already know?

Story Builders

Guided practice is a must when working with struggling readers. They need extensive practice with support in place to tell them when they are successful and what actions they took that made them successful. It is not enough that they provide correct answers. We need to reaffirm why the answers were accurate so students reproduce their results in other contexts. Similarly, we need to tell students when they are not successful and where their thinking broke down so they can learn from their mistakes. This back-and-forth between teacher and student is much like the relationship between coach and player. It involves ongoing, extensive practice with tiered feedback on how to improve performance. Students draw conclusions on short pieces of text, rather than on the entire text at the end of the reading when they are overwhelmed with comprehension deficits.

Materials and Preparation

- Timer
- A story that is unfamiliar to students

Divide the story into sections that you can read in 1 to 3 minutes.

Directions

Set the timer. Read the first few sentences of the story, stopping to draw conclusions about the text. Reaffirm the role of textual facts and reader's knowledge or experience in the process of drawing conclusions. When the timer goes off, ask your students what conclusion they can draw about the text up to that point. Remember to ask them to supply facts from the text to support their conclusions. If students offer an irrational conclusion, trace their thinking with them back to the text. What evidence suggests such an inference? If students draw a conclusion with no evidence from the text, remind them that they have to base their ideas on what the author tells them.

Continue reading but stop just before the story ends. Ask students to compose a story ending and discuss their conclusions. Then read the actual ending and compare it with students' endings. Are the endings similar or different? How do facts from the text affect their endings? How does their individual knowledge affect their endings? What can we learn about the author based on her or his ending?

Focus Questions

1. What do you think happens next in the story? Use evidence from the text to support your answer.

2. Using information from the story, explain how the main character's action turned out to be _____ .

3. Using details from the text, explain why you think _____ occurred.

The Power of Quotes

Referring back to text is an essential way that readers draw inferences, yet struggling readers often complain about the practice of rereading. Reading a passage through one time can produce so many cognitive and emotional anxieties that asking these students to return to the text often brings them to a complete stop. One way to bridge that reluctance is through an activity like this one, which allows students to be creative and hands-on.

Materials

- Cardboard cylinder from roll of paper towels
- Index cards
- Markers
- Tape or glue
- A text that is appropriate for your students

Directions

Read the text. Ask students to draw a conclusion about the text, based on what they have just heard. Have them write the conclusion on an index card and attach it to one end of the cylinder. Then, on another index card, have them write evidence (a direct quote) from the text that led them to draw the conclusion and attach this card to the other end of the cylinder. Then ask students to share their conclusions as well as the quotes that led them to draw that inference.

Focus Questions

1. You can tell from the information in the passage that _____ .

2. If you wanted to persuade someone that _____ is _____ , which quotes from the text would you use? Why?

3. Using details from the text, explain why you think _____ occurred.

Ready . . . Set . . . Go!

Ask students to find a "just there" question—one whose answer is stated explicitly in the text—and most can do so with little effort. If you ask them to draw a conclusion about the text, however, you may see an entirely different outcome. One way to develop inferring skills is to focus on hands-on activities that provide students with a visual support for the abstract nature of inferential thinking. In this activity, students use markers to identify the portion of the text that directly leads them to make an inference. This is an easy way to provide concrete support for the struggling reader.

Materials

- A copy of a passage and a highlighter for each student

Directions

Ready? Hand out the text and highlighters. Set? Pose questions that elicit students' inferential understanding. Go! For each question, ask students to highlight the quote on which they based their answer. Once students are prepared to share their conclusions, and more significantly, their quotes, engage them in a conversation. Ensure that each student shares a quote and explains how each quote led to forming an inference.

The power of this activity rests in several aspects of its delivery. First, providing highlighters allows students to interact with the text. Second, utilizing this structure in a group format builds a sense of community which can be crucial for students who feel that they just don't "get it" when asked to draw conclusions. Third, sharing their responses encourages students to learn from one another and instills a belief that each of them has something important to bring to the group. Fourth, providing multiple chances to practice presenting inferences with explicit information from the text helps prepare students to work independently.

Focus Questions

1. What do you think the author meant by _____ ? Use evidence from the text to support your answer.

2. What might happen next? Use evidence from the text to support your answer.

3. How would you describe _____ ? Use evidence from the text to support your answer.

4. What will most likely happen if _____ ? Use evidence from the text to support your answer.

5. Why did the author _____ ? Use evidence from the text to support your answer.

Explicit Versus Implicit

Recognizing the differences between explicit statements and implicit statements is the first step in drawing conclusions. We need to spend time with struggling readers, emphasizing the differences between these types of statements as well as how each statement can deepen our understanding of what we read.

Materials

- A familiar text
- Sentence strips
- Markers

Directions

Create sentence strips of brief statements from a text that your students have already read. Each strip should reflect either an explicit statement or an inference drawn from the text. Ask students to sort the statements into their respective categories. Afterward, look at each sentence strip with students and discuss how they arrived at their decisions. Throughout this activity, focus students' attention on the distinctions between explicit text and inferential statements.

Focus Questions

1. Does this statement show exactly what the author said in the text?

2. Does this statement demonstrate an inference drawn from the text?

● Text Back-Up

One method of chunking information is to work backward, giving students the answer first and then asking them to identify the piece of text that could help them arrive at the answer. In the case of drawing conclusions, we often scaffold students' understanding of this skill by providing them with an actual conclusion and asking them to locate evidence from the text to support such a statement. Later, students will need to complete both parts of the answer—statement and evidence—but at the beginning, this method of chunking allows them to see the bigger picture and experience success with controlled practice.

Materials

● A text appropriate for students

Directions

After reading the text, list a number of conclusions that a reader could draw from the passage. Then instruct your students to locate evidence in the text that supports each conclusion. As they identify each piece of evidence, discuss how it supports the conclusion. Be sure to encourage students to verbalize how they came to link that part of the text to the conclusion.

Focus Questions

1. What evidence can you find to support the conclusion that _____?

2. What facts supports the idea that _____?

Analyzing Text

Sentence frames are effective because they enable students to see how information is organized and point out which specific piece of that structure they need to add. The frame shows where the information fits, what it should include, and sometimes, based on the information provided in the frame, a hint of where to find that information. Information frames, such as the one shown below, serve the same purpose as sentence frames and are equally beneficial for struggling students, offering them a starting point and a direction about what to do next.

Materials

- Texts that are new to students

Directions

Support your students' learning by giving them one piece of the text analysis of a passage and asking them to fill in the rest. For example, give them a conclusion without providing the textual evidence. Then, using a different text, offer students another conclusion and part of the textual evidence. Finally, with another text, provide them the text evidence and ask them to draw a conclusion. Use the graphic below to frame their thinking and to organize the information you give with the information they must provide.

DRAWING CONCLUSIONS FRAMEWORK

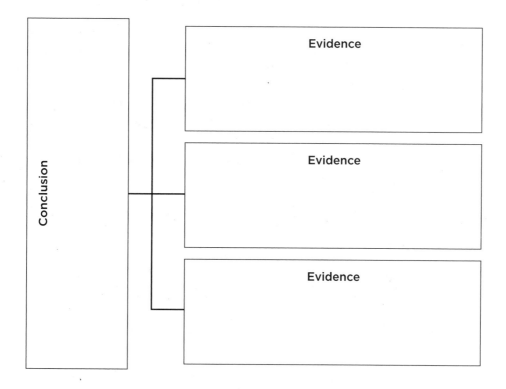

Focus Questions

1. What evidence from the text supports your answer?

2. What do you know about the evidence from the text? What do you think about what you have read, heard, or experienced about this topic?

3. What inference can you make when you think about what the text says and what you already know?

4. Is there more than one piece of evidence from the text that supports your answer?

5. Which pieces of evidence provide the strongest support for your answer?

● Text Trio

Collaborative activities are an essential means of helping struggling readers. These students often see the process of making meaning from a text as a solitary act. To combat this feeling, we have struggling students work with other students. This collaboration not only builds camaraderie, but it also acts as another crucial line of support.

Materials

- A text for each group

Directions

Place your students in groups of three. Each student will have a different task, but work must be collaborative in order for the assignment to be considered complete. After reading a text appropriate to the group, pose a question. Student 1 must answer the question. Student 2 must locate explicit textual evidence for that answer. Student 3 must locate inferential clues that support the answer. Then, working together, they craft a written response to the question that incorporates all three aspects of their work.

Focus Questions

1. What evidence from the text supports your answer?

2. What inference can you draw from the text that supports your answer?

3. Which pieces of information most strongly support your answer? Why?

Text Cutouts

Helping students see the connections within a text can be a huge lift in developing their reading and comprehension skills. Physically taking apart the text can be some of the most powerful work they will do. In the case of drawing conclusions, we especially like to have students look closely at a passage and see how individual ideas support one another. The ability to analyze individual statements is crucial if we expect students to evaluate which evidence is the most important. This activity is a great example of how to "deconstruct" the text and "reconstruct" it with a deeper understanding of how the ideas in it interact and reinforce one another.

Materials and Preparation

- A text suitable for each group
- Sheets of paper
- A marker
- Scissors

Copy a passage from the text. Identify several conclusions that readers could draw from the text and write each one on a separate sheet of paper. Create text cutouts by cutting out individual statements from the passage that support each conclusion drawn.

Directions

Give the conclusions and corresponding text cutouts to your students. Direct them to find the location of each statement that you extracted from the text (this is often a hint as to the strength of the evidence). Does the statement serve as a main idea, or is it a detail from a paragraph with less importance than another statement? Discuss with students how they arrive at their decisions and model for them how you determined the most powerful evidence in the text.

Focus Questions

1. Which statement provides the best evidence?
2. Is the statement a main idea from the passage?
3. Is the statement a detail?

CHAPTER 2

Theme/Main Idea and Summarization

> *Determine central ideas or themes of a text and analyze their development; summarize the key supporting details and ideas* (CCSS, p. 10).

What students need to . . .

KNOW

- Main idea
- Central ideas or themes of a text
- Key supporting details and ideas
- Events
- Summarization

UNDERSTAND

- Main ideas are built through key details.
- Theme is a universal truth presented by the text.
- Theme is a central idea that unifies the text.
- Literary elements (i.e., characters, setting, plot) contribute to the development of the theme.
- Theme typically is inferred—not directly stated by the author.
- Texts may contain more than one theme.
- Both main ideas and themes are developed from supporting details and ideas.
- Summarization contains the essential key ideas of a text.

DO

- Determine the central ideas or themes of a text.
- Analyze the development of central ideas or themes.
- Identify the main ideas and supporting details in a text.
- Summarize the key supporting details and ideas.

Pedagogical Foundations

CCR2 focuses on students' abilities to identify themes in fiction and central ideas in nonfiction as well as to construct concise summaries of content in both genres—which all require determining importance in text. Effective readers are now expected to be skilled in determining importance (Alvermann, Swafford, & Montero, 2004; Gill, 2008; Johnson, 2005; Keene & Zimmermann, 1997; McGregor, 2007; Tovani, 2004; Zimmermann & Hutchins, 2003), as it is "central to making sense of reading and moving towards insight" (Harvey & Goudvis, 2000, p. 118), and nowhere else is it needed more than in Anchor Standard 2. This standard requires the ability to differentiate between pertinent information and extraneous details and utilizing this distinction to develop broad generalizations about a text in order to identify its theme. Theme is significant. Because narrative texts provide lessons about life that are universal and common to all cultures, students must understand that all narratives have a theme. If a reader does not grasp the theme of a narrative, he or she will have lost the power of the story—reducing it to a simple narrative for entertainment purposes.

Of equal importance is the ability to express an understanding of theme in clear written language. For students in the early grades, this means identifying the central idea or theme of a text and producing a retelling (in grades one through three) or a summarization (grades four and up). These written aspects demand that the reader both identify the theme and provide evidentiary support through a summarization of the key events of the narrative. In the case of informational text, students must grasp the central idea of a text in order to be cognizant of the author's intent for the reader. They must also recognize that central ideas can only emerge from tying together key details in a coherent union of thought. Thus, with both fiction and nonfiction, students need to find the inherent connections in the text and appreciate how these connections work in tandem with the author's words and ideas.

Finally, students link their skills in identifying the theme and central idea of a text with their ability to summarize as a means of demonstrating a broad understanding of the text.

● ● ● ● ● ● ● ● ● ● ●

Transitional Steps for Student Mastery

In kindergarten, students need only be able to retell a text, but in grade one students must also be able to demonstrate an understanding of the central message or lesson. Beginning at grade three, students use those skills with specific literary genres. For example, students in grade three look specifically at fables and folktales; in grade four, mythology is added, while grade five includes drama and poetry. A transition occurs in grade four when students begin to summarize the text. The level of sophistication increases again in grade six when students analyze the theme or central message throughout a text and then provide a summary free of personal opinions or judgments. By grade eight, students should be able to identify the theme or central idea's relationship with the characters, setting, and plot. Students in grades nine and ten consider how specific details in a text shape the theme or central idea. At the end of high school, students in grades eleven and twelve should be able to reflect on how two or more themes or central ideas interact and build upon one another to form a complex text.

With informational text, students in kindergarten through grade two identify the main topic and key details with texts of increasing complexity. Students in grades three and five transition from main topic to main idea. Grade four marks the first time students summarize text; in prior grades, they retell only. Determining how main ideas are conveyed and analyzing their development become the focus for students in grades six through eight. Students in grades nine and ten reflect on how key ideas may shape or refine the text. By the end of grade twelve, students consider multiple central ideas and how they interact with one another.

Through the Eyes of an Author

Less able readers often confuse subject and theme. For example, if you ask what the theme of *The Whipping Boy* by Sid Fleischman (1986) is, many struggling students are likely to respond with a general phrase about the subject of the story, e.g., "two boys trading places." While this response identifies the subject of the story, it does not touch on the overarching ideas that allow readers to grasp the lesson of the story, compare it fully to another story, or connect literature to their own lives.

An introductory lesson on theme should begin with a clear definition of the term as well as a review of familiar stories and a discussion of their themes. Fairy tales lend themselves well to this task. They are familiar to most students, and these stories typically have a clear theme that students can grasp.

Materials

- A selection of well-known stories, including fairy tales

Directions

Review the concept of themes in stories with students: Authors write narratives not just to share a good story but also to impart a life lesson for the reader to learn. Practice with several texts to identify themes. Then tell students that they will take on the role of an author. Offer multiple themes (see below), and instruct your student authors to compose a creative story that contains one of those themes. After students have completed their stories, ask volunteers to share their work with the class. Then invite the audience to identify the theme of each story.

SAMPLE THEME SELECTIONS

Hard work leads to success.

A friendship is sometimes tested by difficult decisions.

Courage is not the absence of fear but the determination to do what is right in the face of fear.

Focus Questions

1. What lesson does this story teach? Support your answer with evidence from the text.

2. What is a possible theme for this story? Use evidence from the text to support your answer.

Theme Books

Reading can be such a solitary experience that small groups can provide a much-needed opportunity for students to work collaboratively in an engaging and inherently supportive network of learning. Completing a group project can also be a source of pride and provide a sense of accomplishment. In addition, students can share their individual work while learning from the work of others.

Directions

Provide your students with a set of themes. (See below for examples.) Each student in the group should develop a short story that contains one of those themes. After group members have revised and edited their stories, students should also check to ensure that their stories reflect the chosen theme. The groups should then bind their stories into a book with individual chapters for each theme.

SAMPLE THEMES

It is better to give than to receive.

People have different talents.

Do not put things off until it is too late.

Focus Questions

1. What lesson does this story teach? Support your answer with evidence from the text.

2. What is the theme of this story? Which details from the story support this idea?

Challenge-Response Equation

A narrative's theme derives from how a character responds to a challenge. Helping students understand this equation greatly enhances their ability to identify the theme of a text as well as to appreciate what stories have to teach us about ourselves.

Materials and Preparation

- Chart paper or posterboard
- A marker
- A selection of well-known stories and new texts

Create a display copy of the Challenge-Response Equation shown on the next page.

Directions

Display the Challenge-Response Equation. Model using it several times with familiar stories. Then use the equation as a framework for introducing new texts. Include one element in the equation (Challenge, Response, or Theme), and ask your students to complete the rest of the equation using information from the text.

Focus Questions

1. What challenge does the character face?
2. How does the character respond to the challenge he or she faces?
3. What is the theme of this story? Use evidence from the text to support your answer.
4. How does the character's response to the challenge teach you about life?

Pathways to Theme

Although students enjoy listening to and reading poetry, they often struggle when asked to analyze it or to identify the underlying meaning of the poem and its implications in their own lives. Poems are complex; it's rare for most readers to grasp a poem's meaning after one reading. Poetry demands that we read it aloud multiple times with repeated focus points to guide our thinking. This activity provides that structure while moving students one step at a time through a series of questions that leads them painlessly to discovering the poem's theme and, hopefully, to enjoy poetry in a deeper and more introspective way.

Materials

- A copy of a poem for each student
- A highlighter for each student

Directions

Conduct a shared reading of the poem while students follow along and make notations regarding the poem's content and meaning on their own copy. Begin by asking students to highlight the poem's title, focusing their attention on what readers can learn from the title before attempting to make meaning of the poem itself. After the shared reading,

Targeted Reading Interventions for the Common Core © 2014 by Diana Sisson & Betsy Sisson, Scholastic Teaching Resources

ask students if they can summarize what the poem is about, slowly transitioning them to contemplating the big idea of the poem. In effect, you are guiding your students from a broad summary to a single sentence that captures the essence of the poem. Next, read the poem again, instructing students to circle interesting words on their copies. Lead a discussion of those words. *Why did the author choose those specific words? What do they tell us about the author's feelings about the content?* Also, guide students to understand that the poet's words develop the tone or feeling of the poem. Does the poet use words that suggest the poem is sad, happy, silly, and so on? End the discussion with questions like these: *What do we know about the poem? What is its message? What is its theme?*

The diagram below shows the progression of the discussion.

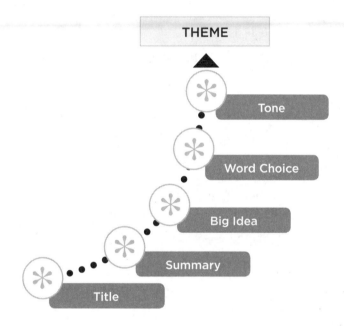

Focus Questions

1. What is the title of this poem? What do you expect it to be about?

2. Summarize the poem. What is it mostly about?

3. Using just one sentence, what is the poem's big idea?

4. Which words do you notice that make this poem interesting? Why do you think the author chose them? Would the poem's meaning change if the author had selected other words?

5. Look at the words you circled in your copy of the poem. Are they fun, sad, serious, scary? Based on these words, what do you think the tone of the poem is? Why do you think this?

6. Consider everything we have discussed so far. What do you think the poet's central message is? What is the theme of this poem? Use evidence from the text to support your answer.

Developing Theme

While it can be difficult for struggling readers to determine the theme of a narrative, the complexity of this task grows significantly when these students must attempt to trace the development of a theme throughout a story. As with most multi-faceted tasks, teaching students to discern the theme of a text requires that we look for ways to chunk information into smaller, more manageable bits. The Developing Theme reproducible encourages students to look at isolated questions about specific narrative elements of a text and then consider how those elements may influence the theme throughout the course of the narrative.

Materials

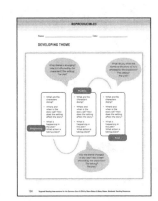

- A short narrative, such as a fairy tale
- Developing Theme reproducible, p. 124: display copy and a copy for each student

Directions

For this activity, we recommend beginning with a fairy tale. This genre lends itself well to this task because these stories are familiar to most students, and they typically have a clear theme that they can easily discern. Read the story through once with students. Then, using the Developing Theme reproducible, trace the development of the theme, one narrative element at a time (e.g., *What are the characters doing in the beginning of the story? Do you see a theme emerging yet? What are the characters doing in the middle of the story? Has the theme changed in any way based on the characters' actions or reactions to challenges presented to them? What are these characters doing by the end of the story? Do their final actions and reactions have any effect on theme? Do you think that it changed throughout the story? Why? Do the characters influence the author's message? How? Do their actions throughout the story change the way you saw the story and its ultimate meaning?*) Continue this in-depth discussion with both setting and plot.

Focus Questions

1. What does this story teach? Use evidence from the text to support your answer.

2. A possible theme for this story is _____ .

3. Trace the development of theme throughout this story. How does it change?

4. How is the theme of this story influenced by the characters? Use evidence from the text to support your answer.

5. How is the theme of this story influenced by the setting? Use evidence from the text to support your answer.

6. How is the theme of this story influenced by the plot? Use evidence from the text to support your answer.

7. Does the theme of this story change in any way throughout its telling? If so, what do you think has the greatest influence on it? Characters? Setting? Plot? Why? Use evidence from the text to support your answer.

Extension Activity

* Rather than focusing on just one narrative element at a time, emphasize the temporal relationships in the development of the theme. For example, analyze all the narrative elements at the beginning of the story, then in the middle, and finally at the end of the narrative.

Five-Finger Method

At the very heart of determining the central idea of a text is the ability of the reader to recognize that details—while interesting—provide only bits of information. The central idea, or main idea, of a text is one that the author continually returns to for emphasis, because it embodies the purpose of the passage. If students feel fatigued from making meaning from a text, asking them to identify the central idea may simply be too much for them to process. The Five-Finger Method provides a kinesthetic, concrete strategy for students by asking them to simply count the number of times they see an idea presented in the text. Most students will not require this strategy, but those who exhibit extreme difficulty in determining central ideas can employ the five-finger method with the promise of success. We have used this method with struggling readers, second-language learners, and special-needs students. It has never failed—not once!

Materials

* A simple text that is appropriate for the group

Directions

Begin by reading a short passage from the text, such as a single paragraph. Model for students as you count the number of times you see a particular piece of information in the text.

* If the author discusses the information once or twice, it is a detail.

* If the author repeats the information three or more times, it is the main idea of the passage.

Students can literally count on their fingers in order to identify the central idea. Reinforce that understanding: One or two fingers indicate a detail. Three or four fingers signify the main idea of the text. After students have had repeated experience with this strategy (e.g., with larger pieces of text, less teacher guidance, no longer physically counting ideas on their fingers), encourage them to continue to identify the central idea using only the premise of the strategy without these supports.

Focus Questions

1. Which sentence best states the central idea of this passage?

2. What is the main idea in this text? Use information from the passage to support your answer.

3. What is this passage mainly about?

● Building Blocks of Central Idea

One of the key tenets of strengthening the skills and confidence of struggling readers is to provide them with a support system. Sometimes that support comes in the form of kinesthetic activities, sometimes in teacher guidance, and sometimes in the visual representation of information. By highlighting the hierarchical nature of text and helping students build from details to a central idea to an overarching topic, this strategy encourages struggling readers to chunk their understanding—one block at a time.

Materials and Preparation

- A text
- Building Blocks of Central Idea reproducible, p. 125

Make a copy of the reproducible for each student. Project a copy on an overhead or interactive whiteboard to demonstrate your modeling.

Directions

Begin this strategy with intensive modeling, teacher think-alouds, and shared readings. One effective way to start is to read one paragraph from a larger passage. Read through the text once, then read through it again, modeling how to build an understanding of the text using the Building Blocks of Central Idea reproducible.

∗ Start with the details. Ask: *What details does the author share? Write down these details on the reproducible.*

∗ From there, draw students' attention to the arrows pointing to the central idea box. Ask: *What central idea do those details support?*

∗ Focus on the top box. Ask: *How does the main idea of this passage explain the topic of the larger text?*

Targeted Reading Interventions for the Common Core © 2014 by Diana Sisson & Betsy Sisson, Scholastic Teaching Resources

As you transition from modeling, to guided practice, to independent practice, remind your students that individual ideas come together to form a main idea, and main ideas tell the reader about the topic—creating building blocks of understanding.

Focus Questions

1. Using information from the passage, briefly tell what the text is mainly about. How do you know?

2. This passage is called _____. What could be another title for it? Use details from the passage to explain your answer.

3. What is the central idea of this text? How do you know?

● Reporters' Notes

To determine the central idea of a text effectively, readers must distinguish between ideas that the author deems important and those that are interesting but secondary. Readers must also be able to differentiate between main ideas (something emphasized throughout the text) and extraneous details (something found only once or twice in the text). The profession that has perfected these skills is news reporting. Journalists can encapsulate the central idea of an event into one concise headline.

Materials and Preparation

- A variety of short newspaper articles with headlines
- A variety of texts in different genres

Cut apart some of the headlines from their articles.

Directions

Lead a discussion of the newspaper articles. Focus on how each headline provides the central idea of the article. Practice reading some of the articles and analyzing how the headline encapsulates the primary points found in the text. Pay particular attention to the kind of information included in the headline. Next, provide only headlines and ask students to determine what information they believe the articles will contain based solely on the headlines. Then, transition students to texts in other genres, having them read a passage and write a headline that demonstrates a clear understanding of what happens in the text.

Focus Questions

1. What would you include in the summary of this text? Why?

2. What would you exclude in the summary of this text? Why?

3. How would you summarize this text?

Extension Activities

✳ One strategy to help students understand the importance of the four Ws (who, what, when, and where) in summarizing a piece of text is through a discussion of how reporters are trained to write articles that are succinct and well-written. To guide your students' understanding, analyze newspaper articles in a shared reading. (See the "4 Ws" activity on p. 31.)

✳ After repeated practice with newspaper articles, encourage your students to write their own newspaper article about a school event. Remind them to include the who, what, when, and where of the story and to add a headline to sum up the story.

● One-Word Summary

Summarizing often proves to be problematic for students who remain uncertain about which aspects of the text should be included in a summary. You can clear up students' questions by highlighting key components of a passage that have the most bearing on the plot and emphasizing the importance of characters, setting, problem, and solution in summarizing narratives.

Materials
- A narrative text
- Chart paper or posterboard
- A marker

Directions

After reading a story, ask your students to offer one word—and only one word—as a summary of the text. From that one word, create an organizer like the one at the right that reflects their thoughts.

Begin with character and then move clockwise to setting, problem, and solution. Ask the following questions: *How does the character(s) relate to your one word? What is the relationship between your word and the setting of the story? What is the problem in the story, and how does the problem connect to your summary word? What does the solution have to do with your summary word?* Then, using this graphic, instruct your students to work from character(s) to solution to write a complete summary.

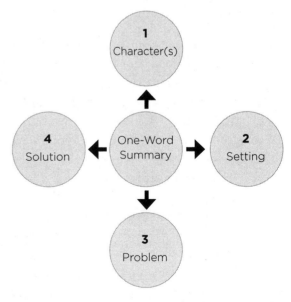

Targeted Reading Interventions for the Common Core © 2014 by Diana Sisson & Betsy Sisson, Scholastic Teaching Resources

Focus Questions

1. Who is the main character?

2. What is the setting?

3. What is the problem?

4. What is the solution?

5. Briefly summarize the story.

● The 4 Ws

We have found that the best way to help readers improve their nonfiction summarizing skills is to provide a frame through which they deconstruct the text, chunk important information, and reconstruct the text in a concise, clearly written summary. All of us have asked students to find the who, what, when, and where of a text. The problem with that method is the order in which struggling students locate the information and try to reconstruct the text to write a summary. Moving from who, to what, to when, to where often leads to a stiffly worded summary lacking in fluency. On the one hand, students show that they can isolate those elements of a text, but the result is an awkward-sounding summary.

The easiest way to remedy this problem is to ask students to identify one element of the text at a time in a slightly different order: when, who, where, and what. Begin with when the information in the text takes place. Next, identify who the subject of the text is, and where the subject is located. Finally, determine what happens. What did the "who" do?

An example of a summary on the topic of the Gold Rush may look like the following.

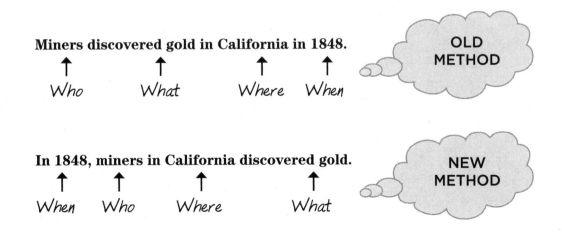

Miners discovered gold in California in 1848.

Who   What   Where When   **OLD METHOD**

In 1848, miners in California discovered gold.

When Who   Where   What   **NEW METHOD**

Materials

- 4 Ws reproducible (p. 126)
- A text appropriate for the group

Directions

Discuss with your students the four main elements of a nonfiction text on the reproducible. Then use it to model how to summarize text. Pay special attention to how to deconstruct the text for individual chunks of information and then how to reconstruct the text to form a coherent, well-written summary. After several experiences working together, provide students with a text and ask them to summarize by themselves with the aid of the 4 Ws reproducible. Make certain that they write a summary from the graphic and that they include all four elements.

Focus Questions

1. What information can be included in the summary?

2. Which of the following could be included in a summary? (Use appropriate details from the text.)

3. What information could NOT be included in the summary? Why?

4. Write a brief summary of the text.

CHAPTER 3

Narrative Elements and Sequence of Events

Analyze how and why individuals, events, and ideas develop and interact over the course of a text (CCSS, p. 10).

What students need to . . .

KNOW

- Individuals
- Characters
- Events
- Ideas

UNDERSTAND

- Authors may convey information about characters through direct characterization (literally telling the reader what the character is like) or indirect characterization (providing clues through how a character looks, speaks, acts, thinks, and feels).
- Individual events function in a cause-effect chain that weaves the plot of a story into a unified whole.
- Characters' actions propel the plot forward.
- Individuals, events, and ideas are connected in text.
- Ideas evolve within a text as the author prepares them to support his or her purpose in writing.

DO

- Analyze how characters, events, and ideas develop and interact.
- Analyze why characters, events, and ideas develop and interact.
- Describe the connection and relationship among individuals, events, and ideas.

Pedagogical Foundations

Narrative elements play a crucial role in understanding and analyzing narrative text (Duke & Pearson, 2002; Dymock, 2007; Herman, 2009; National Reading Panel, 2000; Rowe, McQuiggan, & Lester, 2007; Snow, 2002; Stetter & Hughes, 2010; Taylor, Abler, & Walker, 2002). These elements (characters, setting, and events) remain the same despite text complexity. Their level of sophistication, however, does change alongside the text and its expectations for the reader. Thus, students in kindergarten can identify main characters, setting, and events of a story. What may become more problematic is their ability to understand how these elements interact with one another and ultimately influence the story. This connection among key elements holds true in informational text as well, as students strive to see the relationship among individuals, events, and ideas.

●●●●●●●●●●

Transitional Steps for Student Mastery

Students in kindergarten through grade two focus on characters, settings, and events. Beginning in grade two, this focus shifts to a heavier emphasis on characters and how they respond to events and challenges. Building on this foundational understanding of narrative structure, grade-three students consider how character actions influence the sequence of the story. By grades four and five, students provide in-depth descriptions of characters/settings/events and then are able to compare or contrast these literary elements using specific details from the text (grade five). Each of grades six through eight highlights a specific narrative element with a greater degree of sophistication and skill. For example, the grade-six curriculum looks at plot; grade seven considers the interaction of literary elements; and grade eight analyzes the effect of specific events and dialogue on story development. That concentration continues in grades nine and ten with a deeper reflection on complex characters and, in grades eleven and twelve, with a thorough analysis of how an author's choices affect story elements.

In contrast, informational text expectations revolve around individuals, events, and ideas. It begins in kindergarten and first grade where students describe the connection among these three components of nonfiction writing. Grade two adds the skills of sequential steps. By grade four, students begin to explain the relationships among these elements. Students in grades six through twelve analyze individuals, events, and ideas with closer scrutiny and more sophisticated evaluation.

Character Analysis

As students move into the intermediate grades, it becomes increasingly important for them to develop their inferential skills. One way to do this is by discussing the difference between direct versus indirect characterization. In the former, an author tells readers what to think of a character, while in the latter, the author shows what a character looks like, says, does, thinks, and feels. Both kinds of information help students form their own judgments about a character and make inferences based on those judgments.

Materials

- A set of short stories

Directions

A powerful scaffolding technique for analyzing characters is chunking details from a text and then using those isolated bits of information to form an in-depth description of those characters. To do this, focus on one aspect of indirect characterization with a set of short stories you've chosen. Begin by asking students to focus on descriptions of how a character in a story looks. Have students practice making these observations through several short stories, probing for as much detail as possible.

Repeat this process for each of the following aspects: what a character looks like, says, does (his or her actions), thinks, and feels. As students add each new aspect to their analysis, encourage them to identify one word that best describes each character and to point to details in the text to support choosing that word. The final step is for students to create characterizations based on all five aspects and to use evidence from the text to support their analysis of the characters in the short stories.

Focus Questions

1. How does the character look? Use details and pictures from the text.

2. What does the character say?

3. What does the character do in the story? Use details from the text.

4. What does the character think about in the story? Use details from the text.

5. How does the character feel? Use details from the text.

6. How would you describe the character? Use details from the text.

Character Frame

A Character Frame is a powerful scaffolding technique for analyzing characters. It encourages struggling readers to identify the separate elements of indirect characterization in a text. These students often experience a gap between being able to identify an element of indirect characterization and making the inferential leap to what this detail tells them about a character in the story. Creating an opportunity for students to see these elements in a visual model helps them make a more concrete transition to making characterizations.

Materials

- Character Frame (p. 127) for each student
- A text appropriate for each student

Directions

After reading the text with students, ask them to complete the Character Frame for the main character. Once this information is documented in the frame, students can then make the inferential leap to what all the information tells them about that character. If students still struggle, refer them back to the evidence they listed in the Character Frame and guide them to a rational description of the character based on the details they located in the text.

Focus Questions

1. How does the character look? Use details from the text and pictures.
2. What does the character say?
3. What does the character do in the story? Use details from the text.
4. What does the character think about in the story? Use details from the text.
5. How does the character feel? Use details from the text.
6. How would you describe the character? Use details from the text.

Characters Alive!

Bringing the words on a page to life is a compelling experience for students—particularly for students who grapple with making the connection between literature and real life. As we work with students to breathe life into characters, we know that such experiences can alter both their viewpoint as well as the depth of their understanding of narratives.

Materials

- A selection of short, character-driven stories (one for each student)
- Index cards
- Markers

Directions

Assign one story to each student. Then guide students as they write a description of each of the narrative elements (character, setting, events, problem, and solution) on an index card. Instruct students to come to class on a set date dressed in a costume representative of their character, with their descriptions of the narrative elements attached to their costume. They will then tell their stories through the sharing of these narrative elements.

Focus Questions

1. Who is the main character? How would you describe him or her?

2. What is the setting for this story? When and where does it take place?

3. What are the main events of the story? What happens first? Next? Last?

4. What is the main problem in the story?

5. How is the problem resolved in the story? What is the solution?

Narrative Elements Squared

As readers develop their skills, they are asked to reflect on not just one narrative element in isolation but on at least two, as they learn to compare and contrast multiple characters, settings, or events. This can often prove burdensome to a struggling reader. Comparing and contrasting narrative elements requires the ability to focus on both analysis and explanation. First, readers must have some sort of organizational structure in place to determine how particular narrative elements are alike and different. For example, how are two characters in a story similar, and how do they differ? Second, readers must isolate specific characteristics of the narrative elements, such as what they know about the setting at the beginning of the story and what the setting is like at the end of the story. Third, readers have to consider details about multiple narrative elements and how they are similar and different. A graphic for documenting their findings and conclusions provides an essential means of scaffolding students in this process.

Materials and Preparation

- A short text that has two or more clearly defined characters, settings, and events
- Comparing and Contrasting Narrative Elements (p. 128)

Create three different reproducibles for each group. Write one of the following column heads on each reproducible: Character #1 and Character #2, Setting #1 and Setting #2, or Event #1 and Event #2.

Directions

Before students read the text, give each of them one of the three types of Comparing and Contrasting Narrative Elements reproducibles and instruct them to look at the narrative element they've been assigned. For example, one student would look only at two main characters. Another student would consider two of the important settings. A third student would examine the beginning event and ending event. After reading the text, lead a discussion with your students about their initial impressions. Then reread the narrative, asking students to document the details on their reproducibles.

Focus Questions

1. How would you describe the first character? How would you describe the second character? Use details from the text to support your answer.

2. How would you describe the first setting? How would you describe the second setting? Use details from the text to support your answer.

3. How would you describe the first event? How would you describe the second event? Use details from the text to support your answer.

4. Compare and contrast two characters from the story. Use evidence from the story to support your answer.

5. Compare and contrast two settings from the story. Use evidence from the story to support your answer.

6. Compare and contrast two events from the story. Use evidence from the story to support your answer.

Characters in Action!

Traditionally, we ask students to analyze one particular character in a story. Expecting them to follow multiple characters in the course of a story can be much more demanding and confusing. One way to approach this task is to be explicit about which characters we want students to follow. Then chunk their tracking of the character, using the conflict as the pivot on which they analyze their character.

Materials

- A story with a clear conflict and strong character interactions, such as *Cinderella*

Directions

Discuss what is meant by the problem, or conflict, of a story. Then focus on conflict as you lead a discussion about the characters in the text you've selected and how they develop throughout the story.

As we all know, in *Cinderella* the problem is that Cinderella wants to go to the ball, but her evil stepmother will not permit it. To consider how Cinderella, her stepmother, and her stepsisters interact, we need to identify what each of these characters is doing at the beginning of the story. Cinderella works as a servant in her own home. Her stepmother refuses to treat her as a member of the family. The stepsisters are absorbed with clothes and making themselves pretty for suitors. As the story progresses, the characters react to this conflict in a variety of ways, depending on the sequence of events in the story. For example, what happens when Cinderella wants to go to the ball? (Beginning) What occurs when Cinderella receives help from her fairy godmother to attend the ball? (Middle) What takes place after Cinderella returns from the ball? (End) How do the characters react to this problem and interact with one another at each of these points?

Be certain to direct your students' thinking not only to the beginning, middle, and end of the story but also to what is happening within the context of the conflict. The characters' responses to the conflict constitute their interactions with one another. You cannot discuss one without the other. Adapt and draw the graphic below on the board to help focus students on the process.

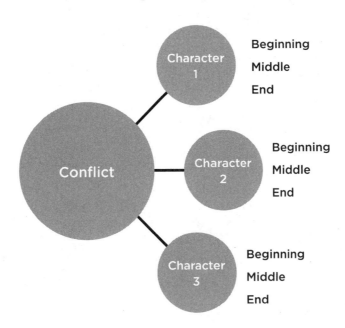

Focus Questions

1. What is the problem, or conflict, of this story? Use evidence from the text to support your answer.

2. How does Character 1 react to the problem at the beginning of the story? How does Character 2 react to the problem at the beginning of the story? How does Character 3 react to the problem at the beginning of the story? How are the characters interacting with one another in the midst of this problem?

3. How does Character 1 react to the problem in the middle of the story? How does Character 2 react to the problem in the middle of the story? How does Character 3 react to the problem in the middle of the story? How are the characters interacting with one another in the midst of this problem?

4. How does Character 1 react to the problem at the end of the story? How does Character 2 react to the problem at the end of the story? How does Character 3 react to the problem at the end of the story? How are the characters interacting with one another in the midst of this problem?

5. How have the characters interacted during this story? Use evidence from the text to support your answer.

● Author's Choice

By the middle grades, we expect readers to plot the growth and change of a character as the narrative progresses toward a resolution. For struggling students, this often proves challenging—especially as more complex narratives tend to favor dynamic characters. While these students may be capable of identifying characters and even distinguishing between dynamic and static characters, being cognizant of character shifts and fluctuating responses to the story's problems requires a great deal more sophistication and insight.

Materials and Preparation

- Author's Choice Spinner (p. 129)
- Oak tag
- Scissors
- Glue
- Paper clip
- Brass fastener
- Pencil
- Markers (optional)
- A narrative text

Follow the directions on the reproducible to create a spinner.

Directions

After reading the story, use the spinner to facilitate a discussion on how the story would be altered if any of the elements changed. Let each student take a spin. If they land on an element that's already been discussed, ask them to spin again or to offer a different scenario. After students have had experience with this strategy, have them spin to select a narrative element and write an alternative story based on that changed element.

 Targeted Reading Interventions for the Common Core © 2014 by Diana Sisson & Betsy Sisson, Scholastic Teaching Resources

Focus Questions

1. How does the story change based on the order in which the characters are introduced in the story?

2. How does the story change if a primary character is relegated to a secondary character? Does it change the problem or solution of the story?

3. How does the story change if a secondary character is promoted to a primary character? Does it change the problem or solution of the story?

4. How does the story change if the setting is altered? How important is the setting to the telling of the story?

5. How does the story change if the sequence of events changes? Does it alter the overall telling of the story or the ending of the story and its central message?

A Look in the Rearview Mirror

Linking characters to specific events in the story is an effective way to facilitate students' ability to trace character development. The framework it provides reduces the abstract nature of character development and illuminates how events shape characters.

Materials

- A short story that has strong story grammar with a clearly delineated beginning, middle, and end

Directions

Read the story, then tell your students to look for the beginning, middle, and ending events as you reread it. Document these events on a graphic like the one shown below. Then tell your students to describe the main character at the beginning of the story, the middle, and the end. Document these descriptions on the graphic. Finally, guide your students in determining if their character descriptions change at any of the three intervals of the story. Discuss why the characters might have changed.

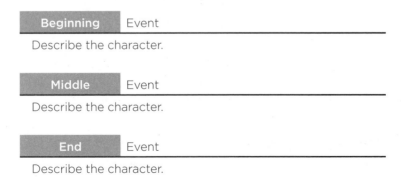

Focus Questions

1. Does the main character change during the story? How?

2. Are the character changes due to events in the story? How?

3. Why do you believe the character changes?

Cause-Effect Chains

One of the most significant features of plot is that a cause-effect sequence of events continually propels the action forward. Able readers appreciate that one event causes another, which in turn causes another. They recognize that events are not isolated occurrences within a story, but rather the events work together to drive the narrative to its natural conclusion.

Materials

- A selection of fairy tales with a clear cause-and-effect structure

Directions

Use fairy tales to model how the cause-effect chain in narratives functions. Introduce the Cause-Effect Chain diagram below. After several demonstrations, provide students with a new story. As they read, remind them to look for causes and their effects in the story. Have students use the Cause-Effect Chain as a framework to help them document their findings as well as to reinforce the visual representation of plot progression.

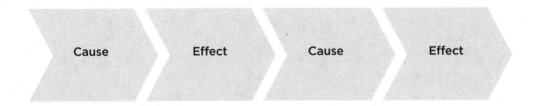

Focus Questions

1. Chart the plot of the story. What happens first? What effect does that have? What does that cause to happen?

2. How is the story resolved? Work backward: What is the cause behind the events that leads to the story's resolution?

3. How do the characters change as the plot moves toward its resolution?

 Targeted Reading Interventions for the Common Core © 2014 by Diana Sisson & Betsy Sisson, Scholastic Teaching Resources

Hot Potato

Analyzing the interactions among narrative elements in a story can be a daunting process. To alleviate the anxiety that struggling students often feel in such situations, we play simple games to make the learning process less tense and more appealing. These games encourage students to think about text, analyze it, and share their findings in the context of friendly competition.

Materials and Preparation

- A small potato (or ball) for each student
- Strips of paper
- A marker
- Tape or glue

Affix a different narrative event label to each potato: character, setting, problem, solution.

Directions

Move your students into a circle and give each one a potato. Ask one student to throw his or her potato to any other student. That student must then explain how the two narrative elements on the potatoes he or she now holds interact in the story. If the student answers correctly, he or she can throw one of the potatoes to anyone in the circle. If the student answers incorrectly, he or she must sit out that round. If the student answers incorrectly twice in a row, he or she throws the potatoes to another student. This continues until only one student remains.

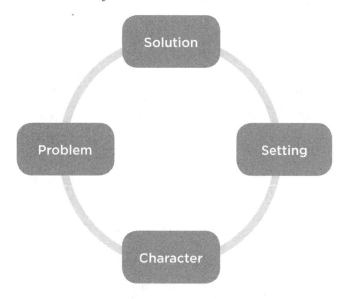

Focus Questions

1. How does setting shape the characters in this story?

2. How does setting shape the problem in this story?

3. How does setting shape the solution in this story?

4. How do the characters influence the problem in the story?

5. How do the characters influence the solution in the story?

6. How does the problem affect the characters?

7. How does the problem resolve itself in the story's solution?

8. How does the solution shape the characters?

● Character Talk

Dialogue can irrevocably alter the plot of a narrative. While some students misinterpret dialogue as an innocuous element of a story that they can easily skip, able readers recognize that the words uttered by characters have immense power. Dialogue not only illuminates the author's intended theme but also propels the storytelling forward effortlessly and fluently. The first step in helping students recognize the power of dialogue is to slow down their reading, focus their thinking on the particular effects of the words, and talk about talking!

Materials

- Short stories with strong dialogue

Directions

Read the story with your students. Then go back and highlight an excerpt containing dialogue. Model for students the meaning of the words as well as what the words reveal about the story. What do they suggest about the speaker? How do other characters react to those words? Does the dialogue influence any future events in the story? Does it provoke a decision? Does it affect the problem of the story? The solution? Continue to work through the text in this way to advance the discussion of dialogue.

Focus Questions

1. What does the dialogue suggest about the speaker?

2. How do other characters respond to the initial dialogue?

3. Does the dialogue influence any events in the story? How?

4. Does the dialogue provoke a decision—either on the part of the speaker or on the part of another character?

5. Does the dialogue affect the problem of the story? The solution?

Extension Activity

* After several guided practices, provide students with a new text. Ask them to locate any examples of dialogue that reveal specific traits of the speaker, provoke a character's decision, or influence the plot in any way.

CHAPTER 4

Vocabulary in Context

Interpret words and phrases as they are used in a text, including determining technical, connotative, and figurative meanings, and analyze how specific word choices shape meaning or tone (CCSS, p. 10).

What students need to . . .

KNOW

- Words and phrases as they are used in a text
- Technical meanings (specialized vocabulary in a given field)/Connotative meanings (words associated with a term)/Figurative meanings (words used to describe something by comparing it to something else, e.g., simile, metaphor, personification, alliteration, idiom, onomatopoeia, hyperbole)
- Word choices
- Meaning/Tone

UNDERSTAND

- Multiple meanings of words and phrases are contextually bound to the text.
- The specific words that an author chooses can affect both the meaning and tone of the text.

DO

- Interpret words and phrases as they are used in a text.
- Determine technical, connotative, and figurative meanings.
- Analyze how specific word choices shape meaning or tone.

Pedagogical Foundations

CCR4 explores the significance of word sense in developing reading comprehension skills. One of the most well-established relationships in literacy is the understanding that vocabulary is inherently linked to reading comprehension (August, Carlo, Dressler, & Snow, 2005; Baumann, 2005; Hirsch, 2003; Juel & Deffes, 2004; Kamil & Hiebert, 2005; Kieffer & Lesaux, 2007; Lubliner & Smetana, 2005; Richek, 2005; Stahl & Nagy, 2006; White & Kim, 2009). In fact, students' knowledge of words is the greatest predictor of their reading comprehension (Baumann, Kame'enui, & Ash, 2003; Lervåg & Aukrust, 2009). Without the ability to identify words and their meanings in context, readers will struggle to read with deep understanding (Artley, 1943; Carlisle, 2007; Fukkink & de Glopper, 1998; Goodman, 1965; Graves & Watts-Taffe, 2002; Nagy & Anderson, 1987; Smith, 1974; Sternberg, 1987). This precept relies on students gaining skills in contextual analysis and integrating that awareness with other meaning-making skills in their repertoire.

●●●●●●●●●●

Transitional Steps for Student Mastery

Developing word sense begins in kindergarten with students answering questions about unknown words. By first grade, students focus on words that suggest feelings or appeal to the senses, and second graders consider how words imbue texts with rhythm and meaning and explore topic or subject-area words found in informational text. Distinguishing between literal and nonliteral language becomes the focus in third grade, while in fourth grade the emphasis is on how to identify meaning through context. This focus continues in grades five through twelve with additional work on figurative language (beginning in grade five) and then connotative language (beginning in grade six). Grade eight also includes analogies and allusions. At a more sophisticated level, figurative and connotative meanings continue to be a focus area in high school, with added emphasis on the cumulative impact of word choice on meaning and tone (grades nine and ten) and multiple meanings (grades eleven and twelve).

Context Clue Auction

Context clues offer one of the most powerful supports for students who struggle to make meaning of complex texts. Incorporating both semantic and syntactic cueing systems, context clues provide an avenue for students to discover the meaning of unknown words—whatever text they are reading; therefore—*practice, practice, practice*! If we do not emphasize context clues, students will not utilize them. With that in mind, follow the teaching protocol below to guarantee that your students become context experts.

Step 1: Complete explicit instruction with authentic text.

Define clues ⟶ Model clues ⟶ Use teacher think-alouds

Step 2: Complete practice activities with teacher guidance.

Small group ⟶ Dyads ⟶ Individual

Step 3: Use authentic text with key words deleted.

Materials

- Drawing and writing materials for creating advertisements

Directions

Teach students these four common types of context clues.

- ✶ **Definition context clue:** The meaning of a word(s) is explained immediately following its use: Geography, *which is the study of places*, is an interesting subject.

- ✶ **Synonym context clue:** The meaning of a word(s) is explained using a simpler term: Pachyderms, or *elephants*, are large animals.

- ✶ **Antonym context clue:** The meaning of a word(s) is explained using an opposite term: I thought my teacher would assign me a huge amount of homework, but the amount of homework was just *miniscule*.

- ✶ **Gist (inference) clue:** The meaning of a word(s) is explained using implied relationships: The weather forecaster said it would *rain cats and dogs*. He was right; it was a heavy *storm*.

After extensive practice and reinforcement with these types of context clues, set up a context-clue auction. Encourage your students to create an advertisement to "sell" the best context clue. Remind them to include the reasons why their context clue is better than the other three. They will present their advertisement to others in the group. After all the presentations, each student will "bid" on the context clue that he or she believes best helps readers understand unfamiliar words.

 Targeted Reading Interventions for the Common Core © 2014 by Diana Sisson & Betsy Sisson, Scholastic Teaching Resources

Focus Questions

1. How can you tell the meaning of the word _____? What context clue can you use to help you understand the meaning? Use details from the text to explain your answer.

2. Read this sentence from the text. What does it mean? How do you know?

Extension Activity

* Challenge students to go on a scavenger hunt to find as many examples as possible of each of the four context clues in the classroom, the entire school, and at home. The student who finds the most examples wins!

Context Clue Master Mind

Able readers use context clues every day as they encounter unfamiliar words. Our task is to stock struggling readers' toolkits with these skills. This will only happen if students can readily recognize context clues in text. One way to foster that fluency is to offer opportunities where students can make independent decisions about contextual analysis.

Materials

* Appropriate texts that contain vocabulary with strong context clues

Directions

Once your students have had enough time to practice using the context clues described in the previous activity and demonstrated proficiency using them to define other words, encourage them to design their own context clue mysteries. Provide them with the texts and instruct them to underline key vocabulary terms that contain context clues. Ask students to exchange texts to ascertain if their classmates can identify the meaning of the underlined words.

Focus Questions

1. Read this sentence from the text. What does the underlined word mean?

2. In this sentence, what does the word _____ mean? How do you know? Was there a context clue? What was it? How did it help you?

Etch-a-Sketch

Teachers often overlook figurative language in classroom instruction. While nonliteral language is difficult for many struggling readers to grasp, it is essential that we expose all of our students to the language that authors use to create vivid imagery and interesting texts. Equally important is our need not only to introduce these skills in one or two mini-lessons but also to ensure that students regularly make use of these skills in their study of literature—anything short of this leads only to a shallow understanding of the text. Happily, with repeated exposure to figurative language, students begin to use their understanding in their own creative writing.

Materials and Preparation

- A story you and students have read during class
- Sketch pads and pencils

Select a character from the story.

Directions

Tell your students to get their pencils and sketch pads ready to draw a mystery character. Begin describing the character you've preselected, telling students to draw the person based solely upon your description. Use only similes in your description; for example, *We are drawing a male who is as tall as a tree. He is as strong as an ox. His hair is as golden as the sun.*

After you have given a comprehensive description—using only similes—ask students to share their sketches and challenge the others in the group to guess the identity of the mystery character.

Focus Questions

1. A simile is a comparison of unlike things using "as" or "like." Choose a simile from our character description and explain why I used it.

2. Can you describe a mystery character using only similes?

3. Look for an example of a simile in the story we are reading. Why do you think the author chose to use a simile? Does it make the story more interesting? Does it change the way you think about the story?

4. Can you create a simile of your own based on a character from the story?

Extension Activity

✻ Retell the character description using metaphors in place of similes.

Targeted Reading Interventions for the Common Core © 2014 by Diana Sisson & Betsy Sisson, Scholastic Teaching Resources

Figurative Language

While figurative language is nonliteral in nature and can be challenging for students, it also serves to make strong linguistic points that can help readers interpret language in ways that literal words and phrases cannot. Figurative language adds spice to what we read, transforming text into something much more entertaining and exciting.

Materials

- Simile Poem template (p. 130) for each student
- A text rich with similes and metaphors

Directions

Review the difference between similes and metaphors: "Similes compare two unlike things using the words *like* or *as*. This comparison suggests that each of the things is distinct and unique on its own. Metaphors compare two unlike things without using the words *like* or *as*. This type of comparison suggests that one thing is the other." Share the examples below.

SIMILES	METAPHORS
She is **as** pretty **as** a rose.	She is a rose.
He is **as** stubborn **as** a mule.	He is a mule.
She is **as** thin **as** a ruler.	She is a ruler.
Those books are **as** priceless **as** gold.	Those books are gold.

Have students use the Simile Poem template to write a poem about themselves using only similes. Then have them do the same using only metaphors. Next, ask students to write a description about a famous person using only similes, then using only metaphors. Finally, present the text with samples of similes and metaphors and encourage students to complete a scavenger hunt, locating all the similes and metaphors within a given passage.

Focus Questions

1. How can we compare two unlike things?
2. What is a simile? What is a metaphor?
3. How do similes and metaphors change a text?

Imagery Match-Up

When it comes to imagery, students know more than they think they do. They just can't always enunciate their understanding. Try working the process in reverse. Instead of asking students to identify portions of text that evoke strong visual images, provide them with a wordless picture book and challenge them to write text to match the illustrations. This activity not only offers a non-threatening context, it also fosters students' ability to use imagery actively rather than simply identifying it.

Materials

- A text that contains rich imagery (narrative or informational)
- A selection of wordless texts that contain rich imagery (narrative or informational)
- Chart paper and a marker

Directions

Read the text you've selected with students. Then chart with them the words in the text that add to the reader's mental images, and then read the text aloud again without these words. How did it change the story? Is the story as interesting as it was before?

Next, present a wordless picture book. Draw students' attention to the visual details of the story, reflecting on how much they add to the reader's understanding of the book. Working collaboratively, develop a text to match the illustrations in the book.

- ✷ For fictional narratives, use prompts such as these: *What does the setting look like? Describe the characters. What are they doing? What events can you see reflected? Can you identify a problem? How is the problem resolved?*

- ✷ With informational text, use prompts such as these: *What do the pictures indicate? What is the book about? What is happening? Where does it take place? When does it take place? What can the reader learn about the subject?*

As a cumulative activity, move your students into pairs and have them select a wordless picture book and construct their own text. Afterward, have each team present the wordless picture book along with the written text.

Focus Questions

Fiction

1. Which words in the text paint a picture in your mind? How do they do this?
2. What does the setting look like?
3. Describe the characters. What are they doing?
4. What events can you see reflected in the illustrations?
5. Can you determine a problem? How is the problem resolved?

Nonfiction

6. What do the pictures indicate? What is the book about?

7. What is happening?

8. Where does it take place?

9. When does it take place?

10. What can the reader learn about the subject?

Denotative Vs. Connotative Language

As students move into the middle grades, the words they encounter in text become more subtle and nuanced. It is crucial to offer explicit instruction in literal, or denotative, meanings versus associations related to literal meanings, or connotative, meanings. Doing so helps struggling readers gain a grasp of the layered implications of even simple words.

Materials and Preparation

- White and colored index cards
- A marker
- Thesaurus

On one set of white index cards, print terms using denotative language, and on one set of colored index cards, write the connotative counterpart of each denotative term. (See the examples below.)

Directions

Give students the denotative language cards. Explain that denotative terms provide the explicit definition of a word, while connotative language refers to words associated with the denotative term that evoke a more emotional response. Distribute the connotative language cards. Lead a discussion about how the connotative language adds color and interest to an author's writing style and makes reading more interesting.

Following this activity, have students brainstorm words of their own with denotative and connotative counterparts. A thesaurus is useful here to provide them with a list of ready words to compare and differentiate between denotative and connotative meanings.

DENOTATIVE AND CONNOTATIVE EXAMPLES

Denotative Words *(explicit definition of term)*	Connotative Counterparts *(words related to term)*
man	gentleman, dude, guy
small	tiny, petite, miniscule

house	home, mansion, hovel
car	wheels, transportation, hot rod

Focus Questions

1. What are denotative words?

2. What are connotative words?

3. How do connotative terms add to the text's meaning and tone?

Connotations—On the Flip Side

Authors use the connotations of words to inject emotional appeal into text. For example, we would look differently at a character who is thrifty from one who is penny-pinching or miserly. As connotations tend to color the perception of both narratives and informational text, struggling readers need to recognize that words suggest nuances that can alter the meaning of passages as well as reveal an author's purpose, partiality to characters, views on the subject matter, and so on.

Directions

Give your students a list of character traits such as the one shown below. Ask them to determine if the traits have positive connotations, negative connotations, or both depending on the context in which they are used. Ask them to explain their rationale in making their choices.

CHARACTER TRAITS

ambitious, bold, careful, confident, courageous, cowardly, demanding, dependable, eager, easygoing, fearless, foolish, greedy, grumpy, honest, impatient, industrious, lazy, mature, mysterious, obedient, picky, popular, proud, quiet, secretive, silly, sneaky, stingy, thoughtful, trusting, warm, weak

---

Focus Questions

1. Does this word have a positive connotation? How do you know?

2. Does this word have a negative connotation? How do you know?

3. Will the connotation of the word change based on the context in which it is used? Why? Can you give examples of how it could be both positive and negative?

Analogies in Literature

Analogies are a type of nonliteral language that present particular difficulties to struggling readers, as they usually appear in text that is more complex. An able reader must make meaning not just at the literal level but also at the inferential and evaluative levels, so it is vital that readers attain familiarity with this structure. Upon reaching this deepest level of understanding, readers gain vivid insights into how an author views his or her subject matter, as well as a deeper appreciation of how all authors convey tone through nonliteral language.

Materials

- A copy of "The Road Not Taken" by Robert Frost (below) for each student
- Several texts that contain clear examples of analogies

Directions

Instruct your students to complete a cold reading of the Frost poem without any discussion. After students have read the text, lead a discussion as to what they believe Frost was communicating in the poem. Then emphasize the analogy of the road compared to life choices. Ask students to read the poem again, looking at the text through the lens of this analogy. Reframe the discussion around this analogy and how it ties in to the meaning of the poem and the tone it carries throughout the stanzas.

Afterward, display the other texts and ask students to analyze the comparisons among them as well as to determine the effect of a particular analogy on the meaning and tone of the poem.

The Road Not Taken *by Robert Frost*

Two roads diverged in a yellow wood,
And sorry I could not travel both
And be one traveler, long I stood
And looked down one as far as I could
To where it bent in the undergrowth;

Then took the other, as just as fair,
And having perhaps the better claim,
Because it was grassy and wanted wear;
Though as for that the passing there
Had worn them really about the same,

And both that morning equally lay
In leaves no step had trodden black.
Oh, I kept the first for another day!
Yet knowing how way leads on to way,
I doubted if I should ever come back.

I shall be telling this with a sigh
Somewhere ages and ages hence:
Two roads diverged in a wood, and I—
I took the one less traveled by,
And that has made all the difference.

Focus Questions

1. What two things is the author comparing in this text?

2. Why do you think Robert Frost chose to compare these two things?

3. How does this analogy affect the meaning of the poem? Would the meaning change if Frost had used a different comparison?

4. How would you describe the tone of this poem? Use details from the poem to explain your answer.

5. Rewrite a portion of the text using a different analogy. Does it change the overall meaning? The tone? Why do you think that is?

Rhyme Time

Rhymes in text suggest repetition without actually repeating words or phrases. They also instill a songlike characteristic to the words, creating a flowing quality to the text that can function as a vehicle for the reader to retain information from the text. For example, think back to this simple rhyme: *In 1492/Columbus sailed the ocean blue*. When we were in school, we learned this to help us remember the year Columbus arrived in the New World. Rhyming words come in many varieties, but whatever form they take, words that rhyme help us remember.

Materials

- First two stanzas of "Paul Revere's Ride" by Henry Wadsworth Longfellow (below)

Directions

Give your students the first two stanzas of Longfellow's rendering of Paul Revere's ride. Read it aloud as a shared reading and draw students' attention to the end-rhyme pattern, highlighting the words *hear/Revere* and *Seventy-Five/alive*. This is a good time to address how authors often use rhyming words to emphasize key points. In this case, Longfellow included the subject of the poem (Paul Revere) and the time of his purported ride (April, 1775) within the first stanza. Continue to focus on the end rhyme pattern in stanza two.

Paul Revere's Ride *by Henry Wadsworth Longfellow*

Listen, my children, and you shall hear
Of the midnight ride of Paul Revere,
On the eighteenth of April, in Seventy-Five:
Hardly a man is now alive
Who remembers that famous day and year.

He said to his friend, "If the British march
By land or sea from the town to-night,
Hang a lantern aloft in the belfry arch
Of the North-Church-tower, as a signal-light,—
One if by land, and two if by sea;
And I on the opposite shore will be,
Ready to ride and spread the alarm
Through every Middlesex village and farm,
For the country-folk to be up and to arm."

Targeted Reading Interventions for the Common Core © 2014 by Diana Sisson & Betsy Sisson, Scholastic Teaching Resources

Focus Questions

1. Which words rhyme in these lines?

2. Do the rhymed words in the text hold any special importance?

3. How does the rhyming affect your appreciation of the subject?

● Word Choice

An author's choice of words exerts a powerful influence on both the meaning and the tone of a text. Struggling students often fail to recognize how the weight of a single word embodies an author's intent as to how readers will experience the subject matter. The subtleties of the English language necessitate that we provide explicit instruction in word choice and draw our students' attention to the shading of words and their implications for content.

Materials

- Passages from fiction or nonfiction texts

Directions

Read a passage from the text. Then ask your students if they can characterize the tone of the passage from the word bank below. Be certain to ask them to supply the specific words that support their choice.

> **WORDS THAT DESCRIBE TONE**
>
> formal/informal, serious/humorous, optimistic/pessimistic, matter-of-fact/ironic, childish/mature, entertaining/informative, bland/vehement, whimsical/realistic, enthusiastic/boring, argumentative/complaisant, joyful/sad

Focus Questions

1. What is the tone of this passage? Point out specific word choices that support your answer.

2. Does the passage contain any words that do not support this tone? If so, why do you believe the author included them? Would you change those words? Why?

Extension Activity

* Challenge students to change the tone of a passage by simply changing a few key words, then repeat with another passage but this time changing only one word. Lead a discussion about the power of a single word to change the very nature of a text.

CHAPTER 5

Text Structure

Analyze the structure of texts, including how specific sentences, paragraphs, and larger portions of the text (e.g., a section, chapter, scene, or stanza) relate to each other and the whole (CCSS, p. 10).

What students need to . . .

KNOW

- Structure of texts
- Specific sentences, paragraphs, and larger portions of text
- Section/chapter/scene/stanza

UNDERSTAND

- Text structure affects the way a reader should approach a text.
- Text structure is purposefully designed by the author to present content in the best possible way.
- Parts of the text (e.g., sections, chapters, scenes, and stanzas) must work collaboratively to create a seamless message; each part of the whole has a purpose.

DO

- Analyze structures found in texts.
- Analyze text elements, including sentences, paragraphs, chapters, scenes, and stanzas.
- Determine how these parts fit together and function collectively to form a whole.

Pedagogical Foundations

CCR5 focuses on text structures and their importance in assisting readers to understand and deeply comprehend texts. It is imperative that students understand that every text they encounter is based on a particular structure or organizational pattern. Recognizing a text's organization signals students as to how they should approach the text and understand its purpose in providing information (Akhondi, Malayeri, & Samad, 2011; Bakken & Whedon, 2002; Boling & Evans, 2008; Cain, 2009; Deane, Sheehan, Sabatini, Futagi, & Kostin, 2006; Duke & Pearson, 2002; Dymock, 2005, 2007; Massey & Heafner, 2004; Meyer & Ray, 2011; Sencibaugh, 2005; Sinatra, 2000.) Identifying the structure of a piece of text helps students determine what is important. What's more, when meaning breaks down, readers can stop and think about how the text is organized and see whether there is something in the organizational pattern that will help them gain a better understanding of what they are reading.

●●●●●●●●●●

Transitional Steps for Student Mastery

The recognition of narrative text structures begins in kindergarten with a simple understanding of different types of texts (e.g., storybooks and poems) and continues into first grade, where students differentiate between fiction and nonfiction texts. In second grade, students must be able to identify the overall structure, focusing on the beginning, middle, and end. By third grade, students work on parts of stories (chapters), dramas (scenes), and poems (stanzas). This learning strengthens in grade four with an emphasis on the major differences among poems, drama, and prose, and grade five highlights how chapters, scenes, and stanzas fit together and form the overall structures of these texts. By grade six, students must understand how these particular parts aid in the development of theme, setting, and plot. This foundational work in the earlier grades coalesces in grade seven with an exploration of how form and structure contribute to meaning. With this understanding in place, grade-eight students compare and contrast two or more texts and consider how different structures affect meaning and style. In grades nine and ten, students analyze how the author's choice of different text structures creates mystery, tension, or surprise. In the capstone experience in grades eleven and twelve, students analyze how the author's choices add to a text's structure and meaning as well as to the aesthetic impact of the overall work.

With informational text, kindergarten students merely need to identify the front and back covers and title page. Students in grades one through three attend to text features of both print and digital media (e.g., tables of contents, headings, bold words, glossaries, icons, and hyperlinks). In grades four and five, students consider text structures (e.g., chronology, compare and contrast, cause and effect, and problem and solution). Students in grades six through eight determine how component pieces of the text (e.g., sentence, paragraph, chapter, or section) work together to create coherence and meaning. Finally, students in grades eleven and twelve evaluate how authors use these components to develop the text's exposition or argument.

It's All in the Rhythm

Rhythm is a significant structural element of poetry that aids struggling readers by spotlighting the natural flow of language. We have found the best way to help students understand rhythm is through music. Start with musical rhythms and transition to poetic rhythms. We recommend well-known songs, such as folk music. The words are usually simple and repetitive.

Materials

- A song that has strong elements of rhythm, such as "Skip to My Lou" or "She'll Be Coming 'Round the Mountain"
- A poem that has strong elements of rhythm (optional)

Directions

Introduce the song and sing it with your students. Then model for your students how to follow the natural rhythm of the music (e.g., clapping, tapping their feet). Lead a discussion about how you know when to clap or tap your feet. Explain to your students that some songs are simply poems put to music. Read the song lyrics, and model again how students can follow the rhythm.

Focus Questions

1. Do you hear the rhythm?
2. How do you know when you hear rhythm?

Extension Activity

* After repeated experiences with the rhythms of songs, try a poem. Remind your students that the rhythm is still there, and encourage them to follow that rhythm through clapping or tapping.

Readers Theater

Readers Theater is an excellent resource for struggling readers. The scripts tend to be inherently engaging and motivating. They also provide short pieces of text with succinct dialogue, allowing students to access it with less anxiety. We have used Readers Theater for years and find that students invariably ask for it during reading time. When teaching the structural elements of drama, there is simply no better text. Readers Theater scripts offer explicit demonstrations of characters, settings, and dialogue.

Materials

- A selection of Readers Theater scripts (see p. 154 for a source)

Directions

Before reading the script, model for your students how to code the text. A sample code is shown below.

CODING KEY

Characters:	Highlight in yellow
Descriptions:	Box
Setting:	Underline
Stage directions:	Circle
Dialogue:	Highlight in blue

Next, assign a student to each of the different codes. For example, ask one student how he or she will know where to locate characters and what characters are included in the script. Reinforce the importance of each of the structural elements. After this preliminary discussion, read the script with your students and have them code it. Try this process with additional scripts until students exhibit confidence and mastery of the elements.

Focus Questions

1. Who are the characters in this play?

2. How can you find the characters in a play?

3. Where are descriptions located?

4. What purpose do descriptions serve?

5. Where do you commonly find the setting listed in a play?

6. How important is setting to a drama?

7. Where do you find stage directions in a play?

8. Why do you need stage directions for a play?

9. Would it change the story in any way if we took out the stage directions?

10. How do you locate the dialogue in a play?

Community Theater

We always cement learning with a writing activity. If students can create original work of their own that highlights the skills we are teaching, we know that they have mastered the content. Having them take a previously read sample of prose and transform it into a drama is one such example. This strategy also provides a wonderful foundation on which to build, allowing students to link the known (prose) to the unknown (drama). There is also the added motivational factor of getting to perform the drama in front of peers.

Materials

- A prose text that has a clear action sequence with only a few characters and a limited number of settings

Directions

Work with your students to design a drama, scene by scene—focusing on what purpose each scene will have, which characters, setting, and dialogue to include—based on the prose text. Afterward, help students verify that they have translated the original story accurately.

Focus Questions

1. What purpose does the scene have? Is it essential to tell the story?

2. Which characters will you include? Why?

3. What setting will you have? Why?

4. What dialogue do you believe is important to tell the story?

5. How will you describe the characters? Are your descriptions true to the original story?

6. Does the drama tell the same story as the original text? How do you know? Do they both have the same main characters? Do they have the same setting? Do the characters have the same problem? Is the solution the same? Has the theme remained the same for both texts?

Extension Activity

* After the script is complete, encourage your students to host a community theater and invite guests to see them perform their play.

3 Ps in One: Prose, Poetry, Plays

A great way for students to learn how these genres function is to try their hand at each one—while using the same subject matter. This allows them to gain a feel for the structures unique to each genre as well as how an author must modify the content in order to follow these frameworks. For example, writing a text about families will differ widely depending on whether it's a prose text (be it fiction or nonfiction), a poem, or a play. How the author treats the subject matter must correspond to the genre. Similarly, readers must vary their approach to each genre and the skills they must use to construct meaning from it.

Materials

- A well-written chapter from a prose text

Directions

Lead a discussion about the salient points of the chapter, summarizing the text and ensuring that students have a firm understanding of its content. Use this base text to launch students into transforming the content from prose to drama. Can they express the key ideas and concepts in a play? What structures must change (i.e., scenes, dialogues, stage directions)? What can they omit? What must they retain? How does the transition between genres affect the subject matter? Next, engage students in the process of drafting the original subject matter into a poem. Ask: *What structures must change this time (i.e., stanzas, rhythm, meter)? What can they omit in this genre? What must they retain? Has the meaning changed in any significant way? If so, how?*

Focus Questions

1. How would you summarize the chapter?

2. Can you express the big ideas in a play?

3. What structures must an author use to write a play? How are they different from prose (fiction and nonfiction) and poetry?

4. What might a playwright omit in a play adapted from a fiction or nonfiction text? Why?

5. What must a playwright retain in a play adapted from a fiction or nonfiction text? Why?

6. What structures must a poet use to write a poem? How are they different from prose (fiction and nonfiction) and plays?

7. What might a poet omit in a poem adapted from a fiction or nonfiction text? Why?

8. What must a poet retain in a poem adapted from a fiction or nonfiction text? Why?

9. How does the meaning change from prose to plays to poetry? Why?

10. Do readers have to change the way they read to understand fiction and nonfiction? Plays? Poetry? Why?

Alternative Realities

We work with beginning readers to help them recognize the individual components of text. By the middle grades, students must understand how these components affect theme, setting, and plot. Each part of the text has a part to play in the creation of these elements. For struggling students, it is essential that they appreciate the power of individual pieces to influence the entire story.

Materials

- A poem, drama, or story

Directions

Focus on one key piece (sentence, chapter, scene, or stanza) of the text. Work with students to analyze how this one component affects the development of the text's theme, setting, or plot. Then lead a discussion about how the text would be altered if that section of the text were taken away. How important is it to the overall development of the text? Finally, encourage students to write alternative sections (i.e., sentences, chapters, scenes, or stanzas). This will give them opportunities to consider how each addition directly affects the unfolding of the story.

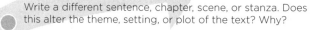

Write a different sentence, chapter, scene, or stanza. Does this alter the theme, setting, or plot of the text? Why?

If you take out this sentence, chapter, scene, or stanza, will the theme, setting, or plot of the text change? If so, how does it change?

How does this sentence, chapter, scene, or stanza contribute to the development of the theme, setting, and plot?

Focus Questions

1. Can one sentence affect the theme, setting, or plot of a text? Looking at an example, are there key words that make such a difference?

2. How important is one chapter in the overall development of a story?

3. How important are individual scenes in the telling of a drama?

4. Must all stanzas work together as one unit in a poem? What if one stanza diverges from the others? Can that change the nature of the poem? How?

5. How essential are individual parts of a text to the overall development of theme, setting, and plot?

6. Must readers be aware of the individual components of text, or can they simply look at the text as a whole?

Soliloquy Stand-Up

Even the term "soliloquy" sounds daunting. What is essential for students to understand is that a soliloquy is simply a character in a drama revealing his or her personal thoughts to the audience. A powerful technique that defines characters and propels the story forward at a deeper level for readers and audiences alike, the soliloquy can greatly influence the meaning of a text.

Materials

- A selection of simple soliloquies
- A previously read narrative text with a strong main character

Directions

Read aloud the soliloquies as exemplar texts to demonstrate their design, content, and implications for the narrative. Lead a guided writing activity in which you and your students construct an original soliloquy based on a character found in the text. Be certain that you choose a narrative that has a strong main character who will lend himself or herself well to an analysis of his or her personal thoughts in the story.

Focus Questions

1. How do you determine what to include and what to exclude in the soliloquy?
2. How does the soliloquy contribute to the meaning of the story?

Extension Activities

* Assign a writing team of two or three students to create an original soliloquy. Then ask them to exchange their papers with another team to determine if they can identify which character is sharing his or her thoughts from the story.

* Encourage students to stand up and perform their soliloquies as a dramatization of the story.

Stable Sonnets

We have been teaching sonnets to middle school students for years. Sonnets may sound sophisticated, but remember that the word *sonnet* is believed to derive from the Italian word *sonetto*—meaning "little song." What middle school student does not like music?

The trick to sonnets, as with every other detailed process, is to chunk it! We begin by modeling couplets (two-line stanzas), then quatrains (four-line stanzas), and finally Shakespearean sonnets (three quatrains followed by a single couplet). When they reach the point of using a Shakespearean sonnet, or English sonnet, students have already had extensive practice with the individual pieces and can put them all together to fashion a sonnet. The second secret is to show students explicitly how each piece of the poem helps develop the meaning of the overall poem.

Materials

- A selection of poems (couplets, quatrains, and Shakespearean sonnets)

Directions

Read the selection of poems. For the sonnets, ask students to label each stanza as either a quatrain or a couplet. Then highlight the purpose of each of the four stanzas as shown below.

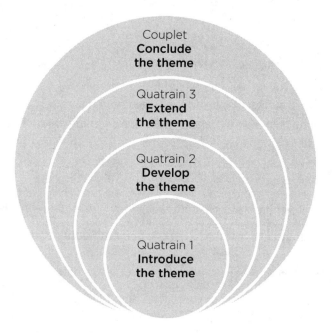

Focus Questions

1. What theme is expressed in the first quatrain?

2. How does the second quatrain develop the theme?

3. In what ways does the third quatrain extend the theme?

4. How does the sonnet conclude? Does it bring about a clear resolution to the theme?

Targeted Reading Interventions for the Common Core © 2014 by Diana Sisson & Betsy Sisson, Scholastic Teaching Resources

A Day in the Life of a Text Structure

Every text that students encounter is based on a particular structure or organizational pattern. Recognizing how a piece is organized helps readers locate information quickly and efficiently. It also helps them determine what is important in the text, so when meaning breaks down, readers can stop and think about how the text is organized and see whether something in the organizational pattern can help them make sense of what they are reading.

Directions

To begin, familiarize your students with the text structures shown in the table below and discuss how information is arranged in each structure. As you model, define, and explain each text structure, connect it to a story from real life. For example, to dramatize the sequence-of-events text structure, you could simply relate what you did the previous evening. Then ask volunteers to share stories from their own lives that reflect that particular pattern. (For students who struggle to grasp the patterns, introduce only one in a class setting.)

MAIN IDEA	SEQUENCE OF EVENTS	COMPARE/ CONTRAST	CAUSE/ EFFECT
Presents information on a specific topic and gives characteristics about that topic	Presents a number of ideas or events in succession	Presents similarities and differences between two objects or ideas	Presents ideas so that a cause and effect can be found

Focus Questions

1. Which text structure do you see reflected in this passage?

2. How does the text structure affect the style of the text?

3. How does the text structure influence the overall meaning of the text?

House of Text

Authors follow specific text structures when writing, basing this decision on their purpose for writing and what they want to impart to the reader. Four major text structures exist across the content areas and throughout nonfiction genres; however, there are certain curricula that lean more toward specific structures in order to better present the information in the most suitable format. For example, authors of social studies textbooks tend to focus on the sequence-of-events text structure because chronology is so vital in an account of historical events. Science textbook authors, on the other hand, tend to follow a cause/effect structure that mirrors the scientific method. Art and music textbook authors often use a compare/contrast structure to highlight various artistic periods and media.

Materials

- A narrative or informational text
- 7 sheets of construction paper in different colors for each student
- Tape

Directions

Talk with your students about the ways in which recognizing text structures help readers comprehend the text better as well as categorize information so they are equipped to retain their learning in long-term memory. Encourage them to preview a text, looking at headings, subheadings, charts, and figures, to determine the structure before reading. This will prepare them to engage actively with the text and be cognizant of what the author wants them to take away from the reading.

Assign your students a text to read. Then have them write a brief paragraph about the text in each of the four text structures: main idea, sequence of events, compare/contrast, and cause/effect. Each text structure should be on a different colored piece of construction paper and labeled appropriately. Tape the four pieces together in the shape of a box without a top. Tape a piece of construction paper with the student's name on the bottom of the box. Tape two sheets of construction paper in the shape of an open triangle. One sheet of construction paper should have the title of the text, and the other sheet should have an illustration about the reading. Once all the pieces have been assembled, you have your House of Text! Sample paragraphs for each structure of a narrative and an informational text appear below.

Example of Fiction (Cinderella)

Main Idea: Cinderella was an obedient girl. She cleaned the house and cooked the meals—just as her stepmother ordered. She did not even think she could go to the ball until her fairy godmother appeared and told her that she could.

Targeted Reading Interventions for the Common Core © 2014 by Diana Sisson & Betsy Sisson, Scholastic Teaching Resources

Sequence of Events: Cinderella wanted to go to the ball, but her evil stepmother would not let her. So, Cinderella's fairy godmother helped her go to the ball. Once there, she met a prince and fell in love.

Compare/Contrast: Cinderella and her stepsisters may have belonged to the same family, but Cinderella was kind, like her father, while her stepsisters were cruel, like their mother.

Cause/Effect: After Cinderella lost her shoe at the ball, the prince said that he would only marry the girl whose foot the shoe fit. He tried every girl in his kingdom—until at last he found Cinderella, whose foot did indeed fit the shoe. So, he married Cinderella.

Example of Nonfiction (The Conquistadors)

Main Idea: The conquistadors are often associated with the phrase, "God, gold, and glory." This is said because men who left to explore did so usually for these three reasons: religion, wealth, and fame.

Sequence of Events: The conquistadors originally came from Europe to explore the New World. After arriving in Central and South America, they claimed all that they found, such as land and gold, as theirs.

Compare/Contrast: The conquistadors and native peoples each had their own cities, cultures, and religions; however, the conquistadors also had guns and horses that made them stronger.

Cause/Effect: In just a few short years, many native people died. The conquistadors had not only brought horses and weapons with which to fight but also diseases against which the native people had no immunity.

Focus Questions

1. The structure of this passage can best be described as _____ .

2. Which text structure best shows how the passage is organized?

3. How would the meaning of the passage change if the author had employed a different text structure?

CHAPTER 6

Point of View and Author's Purpose

> *Assess how point of view or purpose shapes the content and style of a text* (CCSS, p. 10).

What students need to . . .

KNOW

- Author/Illustrator
- Point of view
- Author's purpose
- Content of text
- Style of text

UNDERSTAND

- The point of view in a narrative text affects both what is revealed in the story as well as how the story is told and what the reader takes away from the text.
- In informational text, it is the author's specific point of view that influences content.
- The point of view influences the focus of the text as well as the information it provides.
- The content and style of the text is directly shaped by the author's purpose in writing the text.

DO

- Assess how point of view shapes the content and style of text.
- Assess how purpose shapes the content and style of text.

Targeted Reading Interventions for the Common Core © 2014 by Diana Sisson & Betsy Sisson, Scholastic Teaching Resources

Pedagogical Foundations

CCR6 takes readers into a more intimate understanding of texts and authors' choices. It focuses on how authors develop texts as well as how a simple change in point of view can alter the information they convey to their readers. This shift affects not only the content of a text but also the style of its presentation, which is vital to readers' ability to make meaning from text (Lyon, 1998; Molden, 2007; Simpson, 1993; Sisson & Sisson, 2014; van Peer & Chatman, 2001). The author's purpose for writing a text is equally significant. Students must be able to identify the author's purpose for writing a text (e.g., to inform, to instruct, to entertain, or to persuade). Each of these purposes is unique and distinctive and provides information that shapes the reader's view of the content to fulfill the author's purpose (Ash, 2005; Coiro, 2003b; Davis, 1944; Fisher & Frey, 2012; Freebody & Luke, 1990; Meyer, 1987; Molden, 2007; Pardo, 2004; Paul & Elder, 2003; Ross, 1981). Thus, a reader who is aware that the purpose of a text is to persuade will understand that the author only includes details that support his or her purpose, and should not blindly accept the premises set out by the author in the text.

●●●●●●●●●●●

Transitional Steps for Student Mastery

The initial step in acquiring skills for recognizing point of view begins in kindergarten where students must identify and define the roles of authors and illustrators. Grade-one students must be able to recognize who is telling the story they are reading. This understanding solidifies in grade two when students identify the author's purpose and differentiate among differences in the points of view of characters. In grade three, students contrast this understanding with their own points of view. Comparing and contrasting different points of view found in multiple stories with a focus on first- and third-person narratives and firsthand and secondhand accounts takes place in grade four, while grade-five students become aware of how point of view affects the way in which events are described. Grade-six students consider how authors develop points of view, while grade-seven students study how authors develop and contrast different points of view within a single text as well as how they differentiate their own points of view from those of others. Students in grade eight learn how these different points of view create textual effects, such as suspense or humor, and how authors can acknowledge and react to different points of view or evidence. Students in grades nine and ten analyze point of view through the lens of world literature and explore the use of rhetoric to support the author's point of view or purpose. Finally, in grades eleven and twelve, students analyze how points of view discriminate between explicit statements and implicit meanings, such as sarcasm, irony, and understatement. Within nonfiction, they consider how the author's point of view or purpose adds to the aesthetic nature and strength of the text.

First or Third?

Authors make conscious choices about who will tell their story, and their choices shape the reader's experience. Selecting a first-person narration potentially provides readers with the inner thoughts and motivations of one character. This insight encourages the reader to be more sympathetic and caring about that character—but it remains a one-sided narrative. Selecting a third-person narration makes readers privy to the thoughts and feelings of several characters and gives them a truer grasp of the story, leading them to be more objective in how they perceive the story. Strong readers recognize the distinctions between first person and third person and realize that the choices an author makes about point of view (POV) change how readers view the story. Struggling readers, however, often cannot identify the characteristics of the two POVs and fail to see how these choices may alter the telling of the story.

Materials

- A selection of first-person and third-person narrative texts

Directions

Encourage students to write a story about themselves, e.g., a favorite family memory. Draw their attention to their use of the words *I, me,* and *we* in their narrative. Explain that their story is an example of a first-person narrative, and lead a discussion about the differences between first- and third-person point of view, using a chart like the one shown below. Afterward, instruct students to rewrite the same story through a third-person point of view. Then lead a discussion about their two stories with questions such as these: *How does the story change? Who is now telling the story? Which version is more interesting for the reader? Which point of view do you prefer to use when you are writing? Which point of view do you prefer when you are reading?* Next, conduct a series of interactive read-alouds that emphasize the two points of view. Ask students to identify the point of view in each text and to provide supporting evidence to explain their choice. How does point of view affect the telling of the story?

POINTS OF VIEW (LITERATURE)

First Person	Third Person
The story is told through the eyes of the narrator, who is also a character in it.	The narrator is involved in the narrative and simply conveys the story.
I, me, we	*she, he, they*
The reader learns of events as the narrator does.	The author can share the thoughts and actions of all characters with the reader.

Focus Questions

1. What is point of view?

2. What is first-person point of view? What clue words can you use to determine if a text is in the first person?

3. What is third-person point of view? What clue words can you use to determine if a text is in the third person?

4. If you change the point of view, how does the story change? Who is now telling the story? Which version is more interesting for the reader?

5. Which point of the view do you prefer when you are reading?

● POV Toss Up

Point of view directs our lives every day. We make decisions based on what point of view we hold. On any given issue, there are a myriad of opposing thoughts associated with differing views. Struggling students often do not make that real-world connection. An engaging way for them to see how point of view influences their lives is through this activity.

Materials

- Index cards
- A marker
- A plastic container

Directions

Place your students in teams of two. One partner will represent a student's viewpoint, and the other partner will represent a parent's viewpoint around a specific issue. Create a card for each issue in the POV bank at the right and place them in a container. Let teams take turns picking a card and then debating the issue based either on the students' point of view or on the parents' point of view. After each round, reflect with your students about why each person on the team had such different beliefs.

POV BANK

- Students should not watch television on school nights.
- Children should be in bed by 9:00 p.m. during the week.
- Children should always receive an allowance—whether they complete their chores or not.
- Video games are a waste of time.
- Every student should have a cell phone.
- Junk food should be eliminated from children's diets.
- Children should clean their room every week.
- Students should wear uniforms to school.

Focus Questions

1. What is point of view?

2. How does the issue change based on the point of view of the speaker?

In the Eyes of the Beholder

Point of view is a powerful determiner not only of how readers understand a story but also what message they believe the author is communicating. An effective strategy to help readers appreciate the way that POV can sway their perceptions is to have them put themselves in the place of a specific character and see how it skews their thinking about the story as a whole.

Materials and Preparation

- A story with multiple characters who express widely different opinions
- Sheets of paper

Write a brief description of each character in the story, and his or her inner thoughts and feelings, on a separate sheet of paper.

Directions

Explain to students that they will be reading a new story. Share how the story begins and how the conflict will take place. Do not share more than that. For example, for *Jack and the Beanstalk*, you might explain that someone will take something that does not belong to him or her. Then give a character description to each student. For *Jack and the Beanstalk*, you might describe the characters like this:

* Jack (a young boy who wants to support his mother)

* Jack's mother (a mother who wants only the best for her son)

* A giant (a man who has worked hard his whole life to have money)

* The giant's wife (a woman who works alongside her husband to have a happy home)

Ask students to write a one-sentence prediction as to how the story will unfold, based on what they know about their character. For example, students may suggest that Jack will be the one to take something. They may also suggest, however, that the giant will steal because he wants more money. As students share their predictions, they will come to see how knowing more about each character changes their understanding of the story. Finally, read the story, and then revisit students' predictions.

Focus Questions

1. How does point of view change your understanding of the story? Use evidence from the text to support your answer.

2. Can point of view alter the theme of a story? How?

 Targeted Reading Interventions for the Common Core © 2014 by Diana Sisson & Betsy Sisson, Scholastic Teaching Resources

POV on the Front Line

Point of view is often cited as the most important component of literary analysis, and it is easy to understand why. The eyes through which an author chooses to present a narrative irrevocably alters how readers understand the story and the message they carry away from the experience. For instance, a first-person account provides an immediacy that connects the narrator directly to readers. With multiple points of view, readers experience a broader spectrum of the story that offers a more impartial telling. To reinforce that principle, it is always helpful for students to take a hands-on approach when they begin exploring the concept.

Materials

- A narrative text with a strong first-person or third-person point of view

Directions

After reading the text, ask your students to rewrite the story with a different point of view. Begin the process by reviewing the two points of view, how you can identify them, and the strengths and weaknesses of both. If the author originally wrote in the first person, have students use third person. If the author selected a third-person narration, have students switch to a first-person narration. Remind them to watch for changes in personal pronouns as well as how the information about characters and action is revealed through the change in POV. Ask students to share their stories, and then discuss how the story changes based on varying the POV.

Focus Questions

1. What is point of view?
2. Who is telling this story?
3. What would you include in a first-person POV? What would you exclude?
4. What would you include in a third-person POV? What would you exclude?
5. Why do authors make choices between first-person POV and third-person POV?
6. How does the story change based on the POV used?

Nonfiction POV Across Multiple Texts

Students have traditionally read one piece of text at a time and then moved to the next in a simple, linear fashion. Today's expectations have changed significantly. Now students must read multiple texts about the same subject, searching for similarities among the authors as well as for unique perspectives. Struggling readers find this overwhelming and often flounder when having to decide where to begin and how to hold this information together in a meaningful way. This activity offers students a framework upon which to "hang" central ideas while they traverse multiple sources.

Materials

- A variety of texts about the same topic or subject
- Chart paper
- A marker

Directions

Reading multiple sources will necessitate repeated readings with a focus question in place each time your students revisit the texts. Start by writing the title of each text on a chart and asking your students to read the texts. Ask: *What do the titles tell the reader about the text?* Students should then read each text carefully, considering what the central idea of each one is. Encourage them to think about questions such as these as they read and compare the texts: *What is the author relating? Is the author writing in support of something? Against something? Is the author simply presenting information? Do the individual texts reflect different aspects of the topic? Is one aspect of the subject emphasized over others? How do you know?* Finally, direct your students to group the texts in order of similar points of view about the subject. Then lead a discussion about how students arrived at such a decision as well as why they believe that different authors hold different points of view and how these multiple points of view influence their own understanding of the subject.

Focus Questions

1. What does each title tell you about the text?

2. What is the central idea that the author is relating?

3. Is the author writing in support of something? Against something? Is he or she simply presenting information?

4. Do the individual texts reflect different aspects of the topic? Is one aspect of the subject emphasized over others? How do you know?

5. Can you organize the texts by similar points of view? If so, how?

6. Why do you think authors have different points of view about the same topic?

7. Does reading multiple points of view influence your understanding of a topic? How?

Narrator's POV

As students move into the middle grades, they are expected to recognize that point of view is not simply a matter of who is relating a text, but rather that point of view has a profound influence on how readers experience the story. Indeed, an author's decision about point of view completely frames the text so that the author controls what readers know and, in essence, what they will not know. Able readers grasp this concept; struggling readers need repeated, explicit discussions about texts and the ways in which point of view affects what they take away from the reading.

Materials and Preparation

- A variety of narrative texts
- Chart paper and a marker or an interactive whiteboard

Copy the Notes on Developing Point of View of the Narrator or Speaker chart below to display on a poster or on an interactive whiteboard.

Directions

Use the texts as exemplars, and reflect on how each component in the chart is illustrated in the texts. Over a series of classes, assign students to work in dyads to write vignettes that highlight the various aspects of point of view; for example, have them write a short text focusing on a point of view.

NOTES ON DEVELOPING POINT OF VIEW OF THE NARRATOR OR SPEAKER

- Point of view is built on social, political, cultural, and mental contexts.
- Point of view depends on how close the narrator or speaker is to the action of the story. Is he or she subjective or objective about events and other characters in the narrative?
- The narrator or speaker's words and descriptions are affected by his or her personal interest.
- The narrator or speaker may not be objective; he or she may attempt to persuade the reader.

Focus Questions

1. Does the character's or speaker's cultural background affect the point of view? How?

2. How does the social environment of the character or speaker affect the point of view?

3. Does the point of view have political implications? Why?

4. How does the character's or speaker's mental state affect the point of view?

5. How does the author's use of point of view aid in presenting characters as either protagonists or antagonists?

6. Is the narrator or speaker being objective or subjective? How do you know?

● Purposeful Text

Struggling readers often believe that text drops from the sky merely to frustrate them. They do not typically think about how much purposeful writing and revision the author puts into a text. When reading with students, we emphasize that all texts have a purpose—that the author wants to convey specific information for a particular reason. The more students understand this concept, the deeper their comprehension and appreciation of text will become.

Directions

Review the concept of author's purpose. Students must understand that all texts have a purpose. This understanding is crucial to their ability to grasp that writers have purposeful reasons for writing and that readers must recognize these purposes if they are to read more critically without blindly accepting the words written on a page. Next, clearly explain each of the four types of author's purpose in the chart below. It may be necessary to devote one lesson to each type. After students have formed a solid understanding of author's purpose, model this activity: Begin by telling students what you did during the last summer vacation. Describe your activities within one of the four author purpose frames—to inform, to persuade, to instruct, or to amuse. Then ask volunteers to summarize what they did last summer within the context of a particular author's purpose.

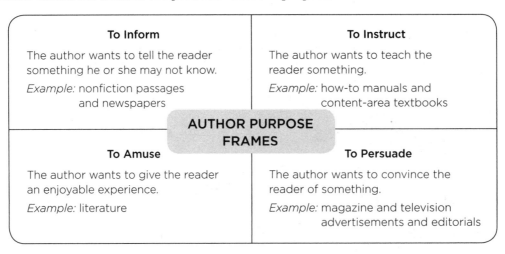

To Inform	To Instruct
The author wants to tell the reader something he or she may not know.	The author wants to teach the reader something.
Example: nonfiction passages and newspapers	*Example:* how-to manuals and content-area textbooks

AUTHOR PURPOSE FRAMES

To Amuse	To Persuade
The author wants to give the reader an enjoyable experience.	The author wants to convince the reader of something.
Example: literature	*Example:* magazine and television advertisements and editorials

Focus Questions

1. What is the author's purpose in this story?

2. The author arranges ideas to develop his or her purpose. What is the author's purpose? Use evidence from the text to support your answer.

What Did They Say?

More than any other students, those who struggle with reading need to make explicit real-world connections to the reading they do in school. Being mindful of that, we always look for ways to make learning connect to students' lives. This activity does just that, focusing on how a seemingly isolated reading skill has implications for students and their daily existence.

Materials

- Three television programs: a news broadcast, a sports broadcast, and a program of your choice
- Three passages from three textbooks in different content areas
- A book or magazine that students are reading
- Chart paper and a marker or an interactive whiteboard

Directions

Tell your students that they are going to look at author's purpose from the perspective of their own lives. Have them follow these steps:

Step 1: Watch the television programs.

Step 2: Analyze the textbook passages.

Step 3: Listen to three of your teachers. Write down what each one says.

Step 4: Examine one book or magazine.

Step 5: Identify which of the four author purpose frames (p. 78) is being used in each of the situations in Steps 1–4.

Step 6: Then create a chart of the results and find the percentage of each author purpose frame used.

Step 7: Finally, write a one-paragraph explanation about why you believe you got the results that you did.

Focus Questions

1. What purpose do the television programs have? How do you know? Would changing their purpose change how the programs communicate their messages or the content itself?

2. What purpose do the textbooks have? How do you know? Are they all the same? Why do you think they may be the same? Could you change their purpose and still retain the same information presented? Why?

3. What purpose do each of your teachers have? How do you know? Why do you think that is their purpose?

4. Which book or magazine did you select to review? What purpose does it have? How do you know?

5. Which example of the four author's purpose do you prefer? Why?

Author's Purpose Portfolio

For students to appreciate the complexity of texts, they must recognize that authors have real purposes for writing. The same information can conceivably be presented in any of the four types; however, an author selects one for a particular reason. When we teach author's purpose, we ask students to analyze their textbooks. They often mistakenly believe that textbooks only instruct. In reality, authors commonly include passages that amuse (to keep the reader engaged and interested in the topic) and that persuade (to influence the reader to hold the same belief held by the author). If students are not aware of this practice, they may erroneously read texts with little analytical reasoning. We also emphasize this same principle in newspapers, news broadcasts, Web sites, and advertisements. For example, broadcasts often transmit segments that are persuasive or amusing in nature—and not only to inform the viewer of current events. In the same vein, we emphasize to students that they need to be cognizant that advertisements are meant to persuade them to purchase a product.

Materials

- Materials for creating portfolios (e.g., loose filler paper that will be bound later, a spiral-bound notebook, a scrapbook)
- Tape, glue, or stapler

Directions

Tell students they are going to design a "portfolio" of the four author purpose frames (to inform, to instruct, to amuse, to persuade). Ask them to bring in magazines, newspapers, and so on, and to identify the author's purpose of each. Then have students cut out the article or story and affix it to a page in their portfolio that is dedicated to that author's purpose. Students can share their portfolios and display them around the room.

Focus Questions

1. One of the author's purposes in this text is to _____ .

2. What is the author's purpose in this passage? How do you know? Use details from the text to support your answer.

3. Why does the author include _____ ? How does it support his or her purpose?

Through the Looking Glass

As critical as author's purpose frames are to readers, they are equally important to writers. In this activity, we transition students from using frames to identify an author's purpose to using the frames to strengthen their own writing. If students are clear as to what their purpose is in writing a specific piece, they can improve their own craft.

Materials

- Student-generated texts
- Sheets of paper

Directions

Ask your students to judge the last writing assignment they completed. Suggest they consider questions such as these: *What was my purpose in writing? Why did I include the details that they did? Were there specific details that were essential to the purpose of the text? Could I have omitted any details without losing the meaning of the text?* Instruct students to rewrite their texts, extracting details that do not support their purpose and that can be omitted without the reader losing the meaning of the text, as well as adding any details that would bolster their purpose for writing. After students finish rewriting, form a round table of student "experts" to examine the revisions and their implications.

Focus Questions

1. What is the author's purpose in this text?

2. Why does the author include this passage? Does it support the purpose of the text?

3. Why does the author include _____ ? Does it support his or her purpose or take away from it? Use evidence from the text to support your answer.

CHAPTER 7

Diverse Text Formats and Media

> *Integrate and evaluate content presented in diverse media and formats, including visually and quantitatively, as well as in words* (CCSS, p. 10).

What students need to . . .

KNOW

- Illustration
- Diagram
- Diverse media and formats

UNDERSTAND

- Illustrations and words work together to convey the story or message of a text.
- Multimedia formats share a common purpose in communicating an author's work but differ in how they are presented and ultimately interpreted by the viewer.

DO

- Use information gleaned from illustrations and text to construct meaning.
- Evaluate content in diverse media and formats, visually, quantitatively, and in words.

Pedagogical Foundations

CCR7 promotes students' appreciation of the written word in both traditional and digital media and familiarizes them with the beauty of the theater and visual artistry. To become educated citizens in the modern world, children need to recognize how varied media function together and serve multiple purposes with one common goal of presenting the author's ideas (Bus & Neuman, 2009; Coiro, 2003a, 2007; Coiro, Knobel, Lankshear, & Leu, 2008; Goetz & Walker, 2004; Kellner, 2001; Leu, 2000; Rouet, Lowe, & Schnotz, 2008; Sisson & Sisson, 2014; Warschauer, 2007). Students must understand the nature of each text format and medium, their strengths and weaknesses, and the ways in which they provide a more comprehensive picture of the author's message than any single aspect can do on its own.

●●●●●●●●●●●

Transitional Steps for Student Mastery

Students first begin recognizing diverse text formats and media in kindergarten when they look at the relationship between illustrations and text. In grade one, students use illustrations and textual details to describe the narrative elements of stories. By grade two, students use illustrations and text to show their understanding of these narrative elements as well as how they contribute to and clarify informational text. Students in grade three take a keener look at the inherent power of illustrations to enhance text, with students in grade four making connections between the usage of text and illustrations to tell stories. Grade-five students build on the work of the earlier grades to consider how visual and multimedia elements add to the meaning, tone, and/or beauty of a text. Meanwhile, students in grades three through five also begin to use and interpret illustrations found in nonfiction texts (e.g., maps, charts, diagrams, photographs, timelines, animations, and interactive elements in digital media). Students in grades six through eight focus on comparing and contrasting the experiences of reading, listening, and viewing texts. For example, in grade six they compare and contrast the experiences of what readers "see" and "hear" when reading a text in relation to what they perceive they "see" and "hear" when listening or watching. In grade seven the focus is on the effects of camera angles, stage lighting, and other techniques specific to particular artistic mediums. Grade eight then draws upon the skill set developed in middle school to consider the degree to which a production remains faithful to the original text and to evaluate the director's or actors' choices within those productions. Students in grades nine and ten build upon these skills by analyzing how subjects are treated in different artistic mediums, and students in grades eleven and twelve study how multiple interpretations reflect a single source as well as evaluate multiple informational sources across differing media formats.

From Book to Screen

When screenwriters adapt books for the screen, readers of the original text often rail against the changes in characters, plot, and ending. Nonetheless, reading a story and then watching the filmed version can serve as an excellent vehicle for students to consider similarities and differences between the versions.

Materials

- A narrative text and its screen version

Directions

Read an appropriate story, asking students to chart the characters, settings, key events, problem, and solution. Then show the screen version of the narrative. As students watch, ask them to document the same narrative elements as they did earlier. Afterward, lead a discussion about how the two versions handled each of the narrative elements as well as what was omitted, retained, and added to the screen presentation.

Focus Questions

1. Who are the characters in the story? How would you describe them? Use evidence from the text to support your answers.

2. What are the settings of the story?

3. Outline the key events of the story. Pay particular attention to the action at the beginning, middle, and end of the story.

4. What is the problem in the story? Use evidence from the text to support your answer.

5. How is the problem resolved? Use evidence from the text to support your answer.

6. Are the same characters present in the screen version? Does this version present them similarly to the book, or are they different? Use evidence from the video to support your answers.

7. Have the settings remained the same in the screen version? Explain.

8. Outline the key events of the video. Do they match the book? If not, how are they different?

9. Do the characters in the video face the same problem described in the book? Explain.

10. Do the characters resolve the problem in a similar manner as the book describes? Explain.

11. Are the book and video similar or different in the telling of the story? Explain.

Mapping the Text

Illustrations are more than simply pictures. In nonfiction texts, they encompass maps, timelines, charts, graphs, and photographs. While able readers make use of these visual supports, struggling readers often feel so encumbered with the written word that they fail to take advantage of visual elements to bolster their comprehension. We always emphasize the importance of illustrations in a text, and then we focus on the layers of information they can convey. For example, maps obviously demonstrate the where of a text. Students, however, should recognize that maps can also provide the when of a text (represented in a label), the why of a text, the how of a text, and key events (represented in a title).

Materials

- A text with a variety of illustrations

Directions

Read the text, and then direct your students' attention to the role illustrations play in deepening the reader's understanding. Focus on each type of illustration in the diagram below, one at a time. For example, look first at the maps in the text. Ask questions such as these: *Do the maps provide us with information about where the events are taking place? Do they give us any sense of time? Maps are often labeled with a time period. Do these maps give any hint about why particular events may have happened? Is there any reference to key events from the text?* Analyze each of the illustration types following this same line of questioning. At the end of the activity, compile what students learned about the focus questions and code the material based on what type of illustration provided the information. Based on the evidence that students provide, follow up with a discussion about which type of illustration provided the most information and which one provided the least.

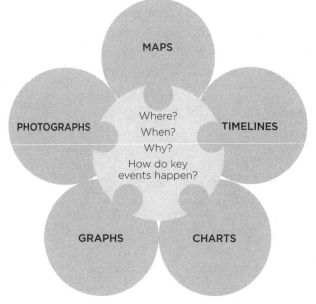

Focus Questions

1. Does this illustration provide information about where the events are taking place? How? Be specific.

2. Does the illustration give any sense of time? How? Be specific.

3. Does the illustration suggest why particular events may have happened? How? Be specific.

4. Is there any reference to key events from the text? Which ones? Be specific.

● Same or Different

Text can be delivered in a variety of methods, including traditional text, visual text (e.g., illustrations, photographs, graphics), and oral text (e.g., speeches). Comparing and contrasting a number of different media enhances students' ability to consider different perspectives about a common subject, broadening their understanding of the topic as well as their appreciation of the different creative aspects authors may take. Each media presentation is different, with its own strengths and weaknesses. The first step is to expose students to a particular medium and develop an understanding of its attributes and what it brings to the reader, as well as how it is unique among other media types.

Materials

- A text accompanied by a visual or an oral presentation of it

Directions

Preface the lesson by explaining to students that they will be looking at two representations of the same work and that they should be looking for ways in which each version adds to the meaning, tone, and beauty of the work. For example, students may look at both a text and visual media (accompanying illustrations, photographs, or graphics) on a given topic, comparing and contrasting their attributes. Use the chart below to guide the discussion and students' thinking.

READER FOCUS		TEXT	VISUAL/ORAL PRESENTATION
Fiction	Nonfiction		
Characters	Subject		
Setting	Place/Time		
Problem	Main Ideas		
Solution	Key Details		
Main Events/Plot	Author's Purpose		

Targeted Reading Interventions for the Common Core © 2014 by Diana Sisson & Betsy Sisson, Scholastic Teaching Resources

Focus Questions

1. Are the two versions the same?

2. Are the two versions different? How? Does that difference change the story?

3. Which version do you prefer? Why?

Gallery Walk

Having students take on the role of artist is an effective way to solidify their understanding of the link between text and illustrations, and the depth that pairing brings to a topic. A gallery walk provides the perfect venue!

Materials

- A story or drama
- Drawing materials

Directions

Read a story or a drama, and then ask your students to illustrate one aspect of the text. Emphasize that they should refer to the text as they complete the drawing, adding as much detail as possible. Then ask students to title their illustration and display it. Provide time for a gallery walk, during which your artists can discuss how their illustrations reflect the written word.

Focus Questions

1. How is the illustration like the text?

2. What text details do you see shown in the illustration?

Reporters' Notes

The modern world overflows with new and exciting media, yet students rarely consider media critically. To activate their thinking and give them a context to analyze media in an objective, analytical manner, we encourage students to act as reporters—to document what they see and reflect on the insights they gain from the experience.

Materials

- An index card for each student
- A short narrative text (e.g., a graphic novel, myth, or folktale) and a representation in a different medium (e.g., video, artwork, or animation)

Directions

Give each student an index card. Explain that their task is to report what they see in each of the media through which a story is represented. They will need to document the meaning (problem, solution, and theme), the tone (the way the material is presented), and the relative beauty (the appeal it holds to the reader and viewer). First, read the text. Then present the narrative in the alternative medium. Using their notes, students will write a brief analysis of the two media and how each communicates the meaning, tone, and beauty of the narrative. Afterward, invite students to share their insights, then lead a discussion on the merits of each media experience as well as their personal preferences.

Focus Questions

1. How is the meaning of the story communicated?

2. How is the tone reflected? Use evidence to support your answer.

3. How is the beauty of the story enhanced through each telling?

4. How are the media alike? How are they different? Use evidence from both sources to explain your answer.

5. Is one medium naturally more interesting? Why?

Multimedia Literacy

In addition to appreciating the merits of different media, students also need to recognize how to use various types of media to help them become better learners. One way to do this is to expose them to written texts, visual texts, and oral texts. Then encourage them to consider how they approach each medium. What are they focusing on when they read? When they watch a video? When they listen? Which skills are the same, and which skills are different, based on the unique qualities of the medium?

Materials

- A written narrative text and two media representations of it (audio, visual, or a live performance)
- What Do I See and Hear? (p. 131) for each student

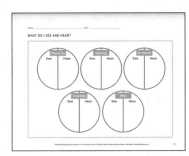

Directions

Lead a discussion about how a reader's understanding of a story changes based on whether the person reads a text, views a video or live version, or listens to an audio version. Focus on the importance of what a person sees or hears in relationship to grasping and appreciating the author's intent. Then provide the two versions of the story and the What Do I See and Hear? reproducible. As students read the story and then listen to or view it in another format, stop periodically and ask them to describe what images they are seeing in their minds. At the end of the reading and viewing or listening, allow time for students to sketch their mental images and then share their work as well as what prompted their images. Next, provide the other media representation and encourage students to observe carefully for differences in the story or in the way in which the audio or visual version enhances their understanding and appreciation of the story. Allow additional time for students to compare the two experiences and reflect on how the various media change their experience of the story.

Focus Questions

1. What do you see and hear when looking at the text? What do you learn about character, setting, problem, solution, and plot?

2. What do you see and hear when listening to or watching the same story? What do you learn about character, setting, problem, solution, and plot?

3. How does the story change based on the experience?

4. Which media presentation of the story do you prefer? Why?

● Poetry Alive!

The last genre that a struggling reader will ever pick is poetry. Even though poetry usually means a short text, struggling readers are often daunted by it and what they perceive as the secret message that only the poet knows. We integrate regular exposure to poetry into our curriculum and believe that hearing poems read aloud takes the frustration of reading out of the equation, allowing students to enjoy the experience and the beauty of poetic language. It also encourages students to see the rewards of their patience and their hard work.

Materials

- A poem with strong visual imagery, such as a poem by Langston Hughes (and an audio recording of the poem, preferably read by the poet)
- Inside Poetry (p. 132) for each student

Directions

Introduce the poem, and read it with your students. Instruct students to take notes on the Inside Poetry reproducible as they are reading. Follow with a discussion about what students took away from the poem. Next, play the audio recording of the poem. Tell students to take notes on the reproducible again to focus their thinking about the poem. Inquire again as to what they gained from the experience. Finish the activity by asking students to decide whether the written text or the oral text was more powerful and how they made that determination.

Focus Questions

1. What did you notice about the poem you read? Did you find any of the poetry characteristics in the text?

2. What did you hear when you listened to the poem being read? Did any characteristics of poetry become more obvious? Why?

3. Which is a more powerful way for poets to convey poetry—through the written text or through their own voices? Why?

Delivery Is Everything

Students rarely think about speeches with excitement. Their conception of a speech is often a dry, boring oratory delivered by a long-winded politician. Keeping that in mind, we never give students a speech to read. Instead, we listen (or even better, watch and listen) to a recording of the speaker delivering the speech. This way, rather than reading empty words on a page, students experience firsthand the passion, the enthusiasm, and the strength of words. It is hard not to be moved by the words of Martin Luther King Jr. or Cesar Chavez. Only after hearing the speech in question do we give students the written text. We find that this method motivates students, engages them, strengthens their comprehension, and—of great importance—entices them to be analytical readers who recognize the power of speeches on people around the world . . . even them!

Materials

- An audio or video recording of a historic speech and a written copy of it (e.g., a speech by Franklin Roosevelt, Eleanor Roosevelt, Amelia Earhart, Winston Churchill, Mahatma Gandhi, John F. Kennedy, Martin Luther King Jr., Cesar Chavez, Barbara Jordan, or Nelson Mandela)

Directions

Introduce a speech appropriate to your students. Once you have provided the context, play or show the speech and discuss the power of the speaker's voice, body language, and facial expression. Then give students the same speech to read. After hearing the speaker's words, ask them to delve deeper into the text to focus on the speaker's beliefs and the evidence he or she offers to sway the audience. Finish the discussion with a reflection on how hearing a speech allows the listener to hear which words are emphasized, which phrases and sentences flow together, and how the speaker's

Targeted Reading Interventions for the Common Core © 2014 by Diana Sisson & Betsy Sisson, Scholastic Teaching Resources

inflections assist the listener in understanding the meaning of the speech in a deeper, more comprehensive manner. Ultimately, students must consider whether the written word can be as powerful as the spoken word.

Focus Questions

1. What is the content of this speech? What is the speaker's message?

2. How does the speaker's voice change during the speech? Does it rise or fall? Does the speaker emphasize certain words or points? Does his or her voice reflect enthusiasm? How do you feel about the subject after listening to the speech?

3. What body language does the speaker present? Is the speaker standing or sitting? Why do you think he or she decided on that posture? Does the speaker lean forward when making a point? Do the body movements reflect the energy of the speech?

4. How would you describe the speaker's facial expressions? Are they static, or do they change based on what is being said?

5. Based on the text, what can you learn from the speaker's words?

6. Which medium is more powerful? Why?

● Critic's Corner

Just as struggling readers often fail to understand that authors write text purposefully, they likewise do not recognize that filmmakers actively choose how they will present written narratives onscreen. Students become more critical of dramatic works when we pair the original text with a dramatic performance, often growing indignant that someone would knowingly change the author's original story. Having discussions about those changes, and why they may have been made, encourages students to be more active readers as well as more active viewers. It is a two-for-one!

Materials

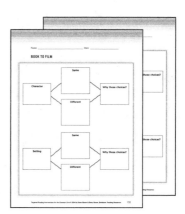

- A story and a film adaptation of it (optional: Locate a second film adaptation for the Extension Activity.)
- Book to Film reproducibles (pp. 133–134) for each student

Directions

Read the story and then watch the film adaptation. Afterward, ask students to organize their thinking about both presentations using the reproducibles. Begin by simply asking students to document similarities and differences. Then lead a discussion about why students believe the writer(s) and director of the film adaptation elected to stay faithful to the original story or why they decided to modify it.

Focus Questions

1. Consider the characters of this story. How were they presented in the text? Was this the same or different from the filmed production?

2. Think about the setting. Did the setting remain the same in the filmed production as it was in the text? Were there any modifications to the setting?

3. The text has a specific problem the characters face. Does the filmed production present the same problem?

4. Reflect on the solution of this story. Is it the solution portrayed in the filmed production? If it changes, why do you believe it does?

5. As you review the similarities and differences between the original text and the filmed production, think about why the writer(s) and director chose to remain faithful to the portrayal? Why do you think they elected to make the changes they did?

Extension Activity

✶ Well-known texts often have multiple film adaptations. To encourage a rich discussion about why people make diverse decisions in the presentation of narratives, find a second production that differs from the initial production your students viewed. For example, there are many versions of Shakespearean productions depicted in widely different time periods and settings.

● Media Ups & Downs

Students typically use one medium for research—print resources. It is imperative that we expose them to multiple pathways of finding information. One way to accomplish this is by having them consider several different media, isolating each one, and then analyzing the pros and cons of each.

Directions

Provide a topic of study for a group of four students. Then assign each student a different medium through which to research (e.g., print, digital, video, or multimedia). After giving them time to conduct the research and take notes, reassemble the group and have students share their findings. As you can imagine, they will come back with widely varying information based on the medium they were assigned. Draw students' attention to their research and how their collected material differs. Then lead a discussion about the strengths and weaknesses of each medium. For example, print resources may be easy to locate, but they may also be less current. Digital resources will be the most up-to-date, but readers have to be aware of the reliability of the material. Videos provide amazing visuals but are often short on detailed information. Likewise, multimedia presentations are engaging and interesting but often lack informative details. End the activity with a debate among each of the expert researchers arguing why his or her medium is the most beneficial to research, with the others pointing out its weaknesses.

Focus Questions

1. What are the strengths and weaknesses of print resources?

2. What are the strengths and weaknesses of digital resources?

3. What are the strengths and weaknesses of video resources?

4. What are the strengths and weaknesses of multimedia resources?

5. Which medium has the greatest potential for research? Which has the least? Why?

CHAPTER 8

Evaluate Arguments in Nonfiction Text

Delineate and evaluate the argument and specific claims in a text, including the validity of the reasoning as well as the relevance and sufficiency of the evidence (CCSS, p. 10).

What students need to . . .

KNOW

- Argument
- Specific claims in text
- Validity of the reasoning
- Relevance and sufficiency of the evidence

UNDERSTAND

- Authors use specific reasons and evidence to support claims in texts.
- Readers must verify that the reasons authors use are valid and rational.
- Readers must determine if there is sufficient evidence to support author claims.

DO

- Delineate the argument and specific claims in a text.
- Evaluate the argument and specific claims in a text.

Pedagogical Foundations

With an eye toward the need for readers to be able to identify supporting details in order to create strong main ideas and authorial points, CCR8 requires students to evaluate arguments in a text. Eventually, students need to use these skills as a means to assess a writer's skill in creating arguments and providing valid reasoning and evidence to support those claims (Fulton & Poeltler, 2013; Gomez-Zwiep & Harris, 2010; Griffith & Ruan, 2005; Larson, Britt, & Kurby, 2009; Nussbaum, 2008; Ogle & Blachowicz, 2002; Stobaugh, 2013). These foundational skills build students' abilities to read text with an awareness of not only what is necessary for a writer to build an argument but also an understanding of what makes effective arguments. In turn, students utilize these skills to become thoughtful readers who reflect on a text's validity or reliability.

●●●●●●●●●●●

Transitional Steps for Student Mastery

There are no transitional steps in literature. This standard only applies to informational text because, with this type of text, students focus on how to evaluate arguments posed by authors. In kindergarten through grade one, students simply identify the overt reasons given by an author to support the points made in the text. By grade two, students begin to consider the "how" of using reasons to support the author's points. The grade-three curriculum makes a significant leap in having students analyze arguments by focusing on text structure (e.g., comparison, sequence, cause/effect). Students in grades four and five build on this understanding to explain how authors use reasons and evidence to support their points. Sixth grade marks another rise in expectation. For the first time, students are asked to evaluate an author's argument and differentiate between points supported by reasons and evidence and those that are not. In grades seven through ten, with increasing sophistication, students assess the quality of the reasons and evidence. Is the reasoning sound? Does the evidence appear sufficient to support the claims? This culminates in eleventh and twelfth grade, when students utilize their skills to evaluate arguments made in seminal U.S. documents.

Evidence Frame

To understand how an author uses reasons to support points, students must first recognize what the points are and make clear connections between the evidence and the main point. For a struggling reader, that task can prove overwhelming. These frames can provide some much-needed scaffolding.

Directions

Using a framed response often helps the struggling reader focus on key points in a text they are reading as well as see the structure in their own writing. As your students develop their skills in analyzing how authors use reasons and evidence to support their points, use the frame below to offer support.

Sentence 1:	This passage is mainly about _____ .
Sentence 2:	The author makes the point that _____ .
Sentence 3:	The first reason he or she gives to support that point is _____ .
Sentence 4:	Another reason is _____ .
Sentence 5:	In conclusion, all of these reasons support the point that _____ .

Focus Questions

1. What is the author's point?

2. What is a reason the author gives to support that point?

So You Claim!

Authors can make claims—whether those claims are reasonably supported or not. The reader must take responsibility for determining if evidence exists to merit such statements. One way to help students do this is by having them chunk the text, looking for specific components. In this case, they first locate the claim, then the reasons, and finally the evidence. This linear approach to evaluating argumentative writing provides a clear structure for reading as well as an explanation of what makes a good argument.

Materials and Preparation

- Nonfiction texts that contain clearly defined arguments and support
- Chart paper and a marker or an interactive whiteboard

Create a display copy of the diagram on the next page.

Directions

Explain that for an author to make a claim about any topic, he or she must substantiate it with reasons that are supported by evidence. Because identifying this chain of thinking can be difficult for struggling readers, use the diagram to illustrate the process. Read the text first, encouraging your students to find a claim made by the author. Reread the text, searching for reasons that the author supplies to support this claim. Complete a final reading, looking for evidence that validates the reasons. This step-by-step process should ultimately lead students to evaluate whether or not the author made a claim that can be supported.

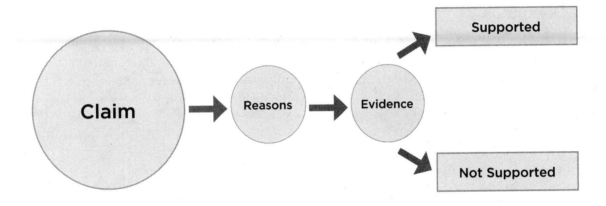

Focus Questions

1. What claim does the author make?

2. What reasons does the author give to support that claim?

3. Does the author provide evidence to support his or her reasons? What are they?

4. Is the author's claim supported or not supported? Use evidence from the text to support your answer.

5. Is the author's claim valid? Why or why not? Use evidence from the text to support your answer.

● R & E Mobile

Abstract connections can best be demonstrated through a visual representation. In the case of the relationship between authors' points and evidence, a mobile makes a strong image for students to hold on to when developing their understanding of how authors use reasons and evidence to support their points. It makes the concepts more concrete—not to mention more fun!

Materials and Preparation

- A nonfiction text that contains a well-defined argument and support
- Index cards
- Markers
- Paper clips
- Drinking straws

Use the materials and your favorite method to create a mobile like the one shown below.

Directions

Read the text to your students. Afterward, ask them to write a paragraph that highlights its main point and the reasons that the author includes to support it. Instruct them to label the main point as well as the reasons. Then provide materials for students to create a Reason and Evidence Mobile that illustrates the relationship between the overarching main point and the secondary reasons that provide evidence.

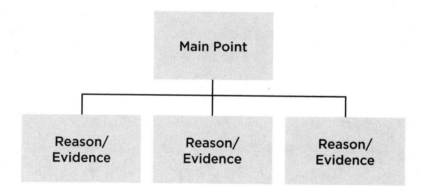

Focus Questions

1. What is the author's main point?
2. What reasons does he or she give?

Side by Side

We like to use partially completed maps to help struggling students. The maps provide a starting point for their assigned tasks and allow them to chunk their reading into manageable parts. It is an easy way to scaffold students' learning and reinforce the structure of texts. If readers experience frustration, they become defeated by the sheer length of a text and cannot recognize its inherent organization. A map corrects that confusion.

Targeted Reading Interventions for the Common Core © 2014 by Diana Sisson & Betsy Sisson, Scholastic Teaching Resources

Materials and Preparation

- Nonfiction texts that contain a well-defined argument and support
- Side-by-Side Maps (p. 135) for each student

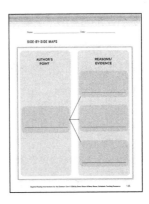

Write the author's point from the text in the reproducible and make a copy for each student. As students progress, write the author's reasons and evidence for another text on the reproducible and make a copy for each student.

Directions

Read the text with your students. Then provide them with a partially completed map to support their understanding of the content as well as the relationship between the author's point and reasons and evidence. Begin by giving them the author's point and asking them to locate the reasons. As they strengthen their skills, provide the author's evidence and ask them to determine the author's point.

Focus Questions

1. What is the author's point?

2. What is the reason or evidence the author gives to support the point?

Adding Up the Evidence

Providing struggling students with structure is a key consideration when building their skills. They face too much ambiguity on a daily basis. To counteract that confusion and ensure they have academic experiences that give them confidence in their skills, we integrate as many hands-on, scaffolded activities as possible. Adding Up the Evidence is an activity that does just that! It provides the claims and reasons, asking students to look at these concrete examples of an argument and consider how claims and reasons support one another.

Materials and Preparation

- A nonfiction text that contains a well-defined argument and support
- An envelope for each student
- Colored index cards
- A marker

Make a set of cards for each student: Print the claims that the author makes in the text on cards of one color. Print the reasons for each point that the author included on cards of another color. Place each set of cards in an envelope.

Directions

After reading the text with your students, give each one an envelope. Explain what it contains and what each color card means. The color provides an additional scaffold so that students begin the activity already knowing which of the statements are points and which are reasons. Ask students to spread out the cards and match the correct reasons with each point. When they finish, review the cards and their correct placement.

Focus Questions

1. Which reasons support the author's points?

2. Do any of the reasons support more than one of the author's points?

● Argument Pathway

Struggling readers can often identify the arguments that an author is making in a text. Unfortunately, they lack the confidence to question the author and to evaluate his or her claims. Encouraging students to be more actively engaged and analytical in their reading requires support. We always tell students to question everything, to never simply trust that the author is right. That independent mind-set can be difficult for struggling readers to adopt, but once they do, it becomes one of the most powerful tools they have at their disposal.

Materials

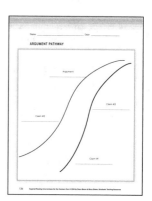

- A nonfiction text that contains a well-defined argument and support
- Argument Pathway (p. 136) for each student

Directions

After reading the text, hand out the Argument Pathway. First, instruct students to document at the end of the pathway what the argument is. Second, reread the text and have students note the author's claims used to support that argument. Third, tell students to look back at the text again and look only for evidence to support the claims. If they find evidence, they should jot it down below each claim. If they do not find evidence, they should cross out the claim as lacking support. When students have finished, review their work and discuss which claims are not supported and why the author may have failed to provide the needed evidence.

Focus Questions

1. What argument does the author make?

2. What claims does the author offer to support his or her argument?

3. Are there any claims not supported? Why do you believe that the author failed to support that argument?

Fact or Opinion?

Evaluating an author's argument requires highly analytical skills. For a reader who is struggling simply to understand the text and grasp its meaning, asking that student to judge the author's words and deem them worthy or unworthy can be extremely intimidating. We have found that rather than asking such a comprehensive question, we work our way through the process slowly . . . one step at a time with a reproducible to offer support.

Materials

- A nonfiction text that is argumentative in nature (e.g., an editorial)
- Fact or Opinion? (p. 137) for each student

Directions

Read the text and then give each student a copy of the Fact or Opinion? reproducible to guide their rereading of the text. Instruct them to begin in the first column, noting specific quotes and how these claims support the argument—which requires them to determine how sound the claims are. Any claims they find lacking sound reasoning or sufficient support of the argument should be crossed out. Then tell students to move to the next two columns and evaluate whether or not the claims that remain are fact or opinion. After distinguishing between fact and opinion, they move to the next step. If they believe that the author can prove the claim, students place a checkmark in the appropriate column and accept the claim. Be sure to emphasize to your students that it is perfectly acceptable for an author to express opinions but that the author must substantiate those opinions. If not, those statements must be removed. After students have reread the text and documented their results, lead a discussion of their findings. Begin with a simple retelling of what students discovered, and then move to a deeper discussion on whether or not the reader should accept the author's argument based on his or her findings.

Focus Questions

1. What argument does the author make?

2. What claims does the author make to support the argument?

3. Are the claims relevant to the argument?

4. Are the claims facts or opinions? How do you know?

5. Can the claims be proven?

6. Should a reader accept the author's argument? Why or why not?

Relevant . . . or Not?

Struggling readers can be overcome by the sheer volume of reading in the middle grades. They exert tremendous cognitive resources to simply construct meaning at the literal level. To help them read more deeply, we have lots of hands-on activities that reduce concepts to their essential form. We start there and build students up— after we've helped them find the confidence to try. Rather than asking students to navigate an entire passage and attempt to comprehend the text while simultaneously distinguishing among irrelevant and extraneous statements, we provide a manageable set of statements that allow them to focus solely on individual statements.

Materials

- A nonfiction text that contains several extraneous, irrelevant details
- Strips of blank paper
- A marker

Directions

Write out examples of sentences from the text that contain relevant details and irrelevant details on the strips of paper. Display the strips for your students to see. Explain what the topic of the passage is, and tell them that they need to pick out any sentence that is unconnected to the topic. Read through each sentence, stopping to decide if the statement is relevant or irrelevant. In either case, question students as to how they made their decisions.

Focus Questions

1. Is this statement relevant or irrelevant?

2. Does it connect to the argument in any meaningful way?

Author's Defense

As students contemplate evidence in argumentative text, they must become adept at critical analysis. As we do when developing other key reading skills, we begin by having students apply their understanding to their own lives. In this case, we focus on their writing.

Materials

- Students' examples of argumentative writing

Directions

Ask students to revisit a piece of their writing that is argumentative in nature, e.g., a persuasive essay. Working with a partner, they exchange papers and analyze each other's compositions. Partners underline all evidence related to the argument presented. If they believe the evidence is relevant and sufficient to be included, partners write a checkmark beside it. If they question the evidence, they write a question mark beside it. After completing their review, partners return each other's papers. Each author must defend his or her argument by providing a rationale for each piece of evidence that was questioned. If the partners come to an agreement that the evidence should stand, they leave it. If, however, they concur that the evidence lacks relevance or is insufficient in its support of the argument, they cross it out. After the teams finish, lead a discussion about what students learned from the process and how it changed the way they understand argumentative writing.

Focus Questions

1. What is the argument that the author is making?
2. Is the evidence sufficient? Why or why not?

Take a Stand

We always try to keep students as physically involved in learning as possible—even in the middle grades. Students at this level spend extensive periods sitting and being inactive. They need opportunities to move and literally put their whole body into learning!

Materials

- A whiteboard and a marker for each student (or a sheet of construction paper)
- A short text that presents an argument

Directions

Give each student a whiteboard. If you do not have a whiteboard, use a piece of construction paper. Ask students to print *Supported* on one side and *Not Supported* on the other side. Then read the text. As you read aloud, note to your students that the author is about to present a claim. Have them listen to the subsequent claim, holding up whichever side they believe is appropriate. Was the claim supported? Was it unsupported? Stop and ask students to explain their choices. Continue this process throughout the text.

Focus Questions

1. What is the author's argument?

2. What claim does the author make?

3. Is that claim supported or unsupported? How do you know?

 Targeted Reading Interventions for the Common Core © 2014 by Diana Sisson & Betsy Sisson, Scholastic Teaching Resources

CHAPTER 9

Comparing and Contrasting Multiple Texts

Analyze how two or more texts address similar themes or topics in order to build knowledge or to compare the approaches the authors take (CCSS, p. 10).

What students need to . . .

KNOW

- Themes/topics
- Approaches authors take

UNDERSTAND

- Reading multiple texts on similar themes or topics builds a reader's background knowledge of the subject matter.
- Authors address similar themes or topics through diverse approaches that allow the reader to experience the subject matter in unique ways.

DO

- Analyze how two or more texts address similar themes or topics in order to build knowledge.
- Analyze how two or more texts address similar themes or topics and compare the approaches the authors take.

Pedagogical Foundations

CCR9 encourages students to visualize, articulate, and ultimately appreciate the universality of literature and our collective human need to express ourselves through storytelling as well as to take advantage of multiple informational texts as a means to enhance their learning on a given topic (Afflerbach & Cho, 2009; Allbery, 2010; Bråten, Britt, Strømsø, & Rouet, 2011; Hynd, 1999; Kincade & Pruitt, 1996; Moss, 2011; Neuman & Roskos, 2012; Voss & Wiley, 2000). Another underlying theme in this standard is the common modes of expression among authors from a variety of time periods and cultural backgrounds. In a world of ever-shrinking boundaries, comparing and contrasting multiple texts allows students to view the world through a more intimate lens and to observe what makes us more alike than different (Colby & Lyon, 2004; Ebe, 2010; Kruse, 2001; Kuzminski, 2002; Landt, 2006; Louie, 2011; Santoro, Chard, Howard, & Baker, 2008; Taylor, 2000).

●●●●●●●●●●●

Transitional Steps for Student Mastery

Students in kindergarten and grade one focus on comparing and contrasting characters and experiences in stories. In kindergarten, emphasis is given to characters in familiar stories, and in grade one, more attention is given to the experiences of the characters. In grade two, students look at multiple versions of the same story; for example, the number of Cinderella stories from countries spanning the globe. Story elements—theme, setting, and plot— become the focus in grades three through five, with book series highlighted in grade three; stories, myths, and traditional literature from different cultures in grade four; and stories from a single genre in grade five. The grade-six curriculum emphasizes comparing and contrasting genres, while in grade seven students compare and contrast a fictional portrayal of historical accounts. Students in grade eight attend to how modern works of fiction draw on themes, patterns of events, and character types derived from traditional texts, such as mythology, traditional tales, and religious works. This focus continues in grades nine and ten, in which students reflect on how authors transform source materials. At the end of high school, students in grades eleven and twelve devote their time to the works of eighteenth-, nineteenth-, and early-twentieth-century American literature with an emphasis on how multiple texts from the same time period treat similar themes or topics.

When reading informational texts, students in kindergarten through grade three focus their reading skills on the identification and comparison of multiple texts. In grade four, students use this integration of information in order to read or write about the topic themselves. Grade five marks the first year when students read more than two texts. This expectation builds in sixth, seventh, and eighth grades, when they begin to analyze these approaches, culminating in grades nine through twelve with an evaluation of seminal fiction and nonfiction works.

Targeted Reading Interventions for the Common Core © 2014 by Diana Sisson & Betsy Sisson, Scholastic Teaching Resources

Theme Studies

You have no doubt heard of author studies, and maybe even genre studies, but you may not have heard of theme studies. We use these for the same reasons as the other two: to provide a framework that students can use to see the structure of their readings. It also gives them a place to "hang" new learning and be supported by the comforting predictability that this framework provides.

Materials

- Stories that are new to students and that contain a strong theme

Directions

Focus on three specific themes for your students; for example, reward for goodness, the quest, and punishment for evil. Describe the themes and provide examples from stories, movies, and television programs. Next, tell students that as they read a new story, their task is to determine which of the three themes characterizes the story. As they read, stop and review the characteristics of each theme and how the story relates to a particular theme. Repeat with other stories.

Focus Questions

1. What is theme?
2. What is the theme of this story?
3. How are the themes of the stories similar?
4. How are the themes of the stories different?

Stories Around the World

Pourquoi tales are traditional stories that offer a fanciful explanation for some aspect of the natural world. *How the Zebra Got Its Stripes, How the Giraffe Got Its Spots, How the Camel Got His Hump,* and *How the Elephant Got His Trunk* are just a few of the great pourquoi stories your students can read. Students love these short, simple texts and their fun explanations for why things are the way they are, and they always ask for more!

Materials

- A collection of pourquoi tales from around the world
- Chart paper and a marker

Directions

Read a selection of pourquoi tales. Focus on a specific topic. For example, select several stories about animals. For each one, chart their similarities and differences in four categories: country of origin, the animals in the story, the problem they face, and how that problem creates a change in appearance or behavior for one of the animals (see below).

Pourquoi Tale	Country of Origin	Animals in Story	Animals' Problem	Change in Appearance or Behavior

Focus Questions

1. Who are the animal characters in this tale?

2. What is the problem in the story?

3. Does the problem facing the animals create a change in appearance? If so, how?

4. Does the problem facing the animals create a change in behavior? If so, how?

5. How do the animals in the tale reflect the country from which the tale came? Are these the kind of animals you would expect to find in this country?

6. How does the problem relate to the country from which the tale came?

7. How does the solution relate to the country from which the tale came?

● Genre Studies

Comparing and contrasting themes within the context of genre can be exciting. Before we move to texts, we have a conversation about common themes in movie and television. Ask a student about the theme of good versus evil. *How is that handled in science fiction? How about mystery? Is it different in fairy tales? What about fantasy? Realistic fiction? Think about all the different genres you watch. Do the genres treat the themes differently?* Definitely—but they also share some strong similarities. Try this discussion as a starting point and then try it with a text. We guarantee it will get your students enthusiastic about theme!

Materials

- A selection of fiction texts of different genres

Directions

Provide students with multiple exposures to various genres. Each time they read a story, highlight its theme. After students gain proficiency in identifying several themes, introduce texts that share these themes and compare and contrast how the stories treat different aspects of the theme. Here is a list of generic themes you might consider:

* Acceptance
* The quest
* Family
* Friendship
* Good versus evil
* Greed as a downfall
* Growing up
* Love
* Overcoming adversity
* Responsibility

Focus Questions

1. What is theme?

2. What is the theme of this story? How do you know?

3. How do these two stories teach the same lesson? How are they similar? How are they different?

4. Why do you think the two stories are similar? Why are they different?

5. What can we learn about the author's way of life based on the way they chose to teach their lesson?

Genre Matrix

Each genre has certain aspects that make it unique. By isolating types of genres according to their narrative elements, genres become easier to identify. We always encourage students to be aware of these characteristics, because this makes texts easier to comprehend and encourages students to look for ways that these narrative elements play out in specific stories. This is a great way for students to begin considering how different genres approach themes and topics.

Materials and Preparation

- Genre Matrix (below)
- Chart paper and a marker or an interactive whiteboard
- A collection of literature

Create a display copy of the Genre Matrix.

Directions

As you work with your students to help them understand how different genres make use of themes and topics, use the matrix below to guide your discussions. As students read literature, keep this chart nearby so they can refer to it for clues about genre characteristics.

GENRE MATRIX

	CHARACTERS	SETTING	PROBLEM	SOLUTION
Fantasy	Fictional but behave in ways that are realistic in a fantasy setting	Usually in contemporary times in a realistic place	Problem based on supernatural events	Often resolved through supernatural forces
Folktales	Flat characters who are all good or all bad	Set in the past, as in "long, long ago"	Problem based on magical happenings	Resolved through magic
Historical Fiction	May be a combination of fictional or real, but all behave realistically	Set in a specific time period in the past, in a specific historical location	Conflict realistic to the time period with both real and fictional events combined	Realistic to the time period
Mystery	Involved in some sort of mystery or puzzle	Set in realistic time and place	Puzzle or mystery to be solved	Resolved through a credible solution to the puzzle
Realistic Fiction	Fictional but behave realistically	Set in contemporary times in a place common to this time period	Character faces a conflict	Character solves conflict
Science Fiction	Fictional but makes sense in a science fiction setting	Often set in present or future time period, at a location believed to exist	Problem based in science	Problem resolved by science

 Targeted Reading Interventions for the Common Core © 2014 by Diana Sisson & Betsy Sisson, Scholastic Teaching Resources

Focus Questions

1. What genre is this? How can you tell?

2. How is this genre similar to the _____ genre with the theme of _____?

3. How is this genre different from the _____ genre with the theme of _____?

4. How are the topics alike and different?

● Mythology Mix-Up

Many students do not realize that authors, especially fiction writers, build off the work of others. By providing students with opportunities to trace common themes, event patterns, and character types in literature, you can broaden their appreciation for literature, illuminate the inherent connections among literary texts, and show your students that everything old is new again!

Materials

- A classic work of literature, such as a myth or fairy tale for one group
- A graphic novel based on the selected text for one group
- A dramatization of the selected text for one group

Directions

Form expert groups in the following topics—original text, graphic novel, and dramatized version. Although all the students will study the same narrative, each of the expert groups will focus on one medium that tells the story. For example, one group would read the original Heracles myth; the second group would read the Heracles myth in a graphic novel; the third group would watch a dramatized version of the story. After each expert group has completed its task, the groups come together to "debrief" what they learned and ways in which the story changed from ancient to modern times.

Focus Questions

1. How would you describe the character in the original text?

2. Does the character change in any significant way in the modern text? Why do you think there are such similarities?

3. Does the character change substantially in the dramatized version? How do you explain that?

4. Why do you believe that this character type remains consistent, regardless of the format?

5. How else is this character type used? Have you seen similar characters in other stories and genres? Why do you think authors rely on certain character types this way?

● Character Quest

Many of our favorite character types derive from ancient myths and traditional stories. Students may not realize that the heroes and villains in the books they read can be characterized into archetypes, but when they come to this understanding, their facility with literature and, more important, their appreciation for it, increases exponentially. This activity fulfills two key purposes: It provides students with an awareness that archetypes exist in literature, and it encourages them to identify archetypes in the stories they read and they write.

Directions

Explain to your students that characters often fall into common types. If we can identify these types, then we can predict how they may behave and interact with other characters. Discuss each of the archetypes. Then send students off on a "character quest." Can they locate a hero in any of the stories that they have read recently? A villain? A mentor? An ally or a sidekick to the hero? A trickster? After students complete their quest, discuss how they identified the archetypes.

Focus Questions

1. Is there a hero in the story? How do you know? What does he or she do that makes this character a hero?

2. Is there a villain in the story? How do you know? What does he or she do that makes this character a villain?

3. Is there a mentor in the story? How do you know? What does he or she do that makes this character a mentor?

4. Is there an ally or a sidekick in the story? How do you know? What does he or she do that makes this character an ally or sidekick?

5. Is there a trickster in the story? How do you know? What does he or she do that makes this character a trickster?

6. Do the characters behave according to their type? Use evidence to support your answer.

7. How would you predict that these characters would behave if the story continued?

Nonfiction Genre . . . Same But Different

While students become familiar with the characteristics of various literary genres, they also need to develop skills to examine how informational texts from different nonfiction genres take varied approaches to particular concepts or topics. First, we teach students what constitutes a genre, then we demonstrate how the genre in which the content is presented influences the reader's understanding.

Materials

- Two texts from different genres with similar topics but different approaches
- Chart paper and markers

Directions

As students read the texts, have them chart their similarities and differences between the content. Reinforce that while the texts share commonalities in content, each text is unique. Here are some examples of different nonfiction genres.

SAMPLES OF NONFICTION GENRE TYPES

Autobiography	Journal
Biography	Letter
Diary	Memoir
Essay	

Focus Questions

1. What is the topic of these texts?
2. How are the texts similar? Use evidence from the texts to support your answer.
3. How are the texts different? Use evidence from the texts to support your answer.

Genre Jam

Genre Jams are a fun way to practice identifying both literary and nonfiction genres. They provide an authentic purpose as well as giving students the opportunity to get up, move around, talk to one another, and find success . . . one book at a time!

Materials

- A stack of books for each student

Directions

Ask students to determine the genre of each book in their stack based on three components: (1) the title of the book, (2) the front cover illustration, and (3) the back cover summary. Explain that the title often gives the reader a hint about the problem, the front cover illustration provides insight into the characters and setting, and the back cover summary offers a glimpse at the plot. Taken together, these three clues enable the reader to predict the genre of a book before beginning to read. Then ask students to sort their books by genre. (You may want to label and organize individual genre areas in the classroom before students begin to sort.)

Focus Questions

1. What does the title tell you about the book?
2. What does the front cover illustration show? Does it provide any clue about the genre of the story?
3. What does the summary on the back cover say? Does the plot suggest a particular genre?
4. Look at all three clues. What do you think the genre of this book is? Why?

Extension Activities

* Ask students to trade their organized books with a partner for a quick "quality control" check.
* Have students select one book from their stack and explain how they identified its genre.
* Use a Genre Jam to organize your classroom library.

Genre Survey

Getting students out of the classroom and into the world to discuss books can be a challenge. We like to ask students to conduct interviews as a way to accomplish this. It puts them in a position of being an expert about the topic, makes the topic relevant, and creates a rich dialogue both in and out of the classroom.

Materials

* Paper and pens or pencils

Directions

Ask students to interview ten people (e.g., students, teachers, school administrators, parents, family members) about their beliefs regarding literary and nonfiction genres with questions such as these:

* *What is your favorite genre? Why?*

* *What is your least favorite genre? Why do you dislike it?*

* *Do you have a different favorite genre for reading than for movies and television? If so, what is it?*

* *What do you think the most popular genre today is? Why do you think so?*

* *Do you believe people's preferences for genre change based on age? Why?*

After they have collected all their data, students should chart the results. Lead a discussion on the findings and what they reveal about people's preferences and the popularity of specific genres.

Focus Questions

1. What is the most common preferred genre? What reasons do the participants give?

2. What is the least preferred genre? What reasons do the participants give?

3. Do the preferences change based on whether participants read the stories or watched them? Why do you think that was the result?

4. What do the participants believe is the most preferred genre today? Why do you think that is their answer?

5. According to participants, does age make a difference in genre? Do you agree or disagree? Why?

6. Are you surprised by any of your results? Why?

7. Do the genres and related themes discussed in your interviews have anything in common? If so, what?

● Eyes on History

Historical fiction provides a fascinating glimpse into the past, but we want to ensure that our students can read critically and evaluate how faithful the fictional account is to the actual time period it depicts. Quality historical fiction can transform what many young people perceive as dry and boring into something exciting that relates to their own lives. Poor-quality historical fiction might lead readers to mistake an inaccurate portrayal of history for truth. Our task is to make certain that students are cognizant of these issues when they are reading.

Materials

* A nonfiction selection about a particular time in history for each pair
* A historical fiction selection about the same time period for each pair

Directions

Assign the task of reading the nonfiction selection to one partner. Ask the other partner to read the historical fiction selection. Afterward, give pairs time to collaborate on how the two accounts are similar and dissimilar. Working together, they will write a compare/contrast essay highlighting their findings.

Focus Questions

1. What happens in the time period that you read about?

2. How is the information in the nonfiction text different from the fictional account?

3. Why do you think the fictionalized account differs?

4. Does the fictionalized account depart from what you know to be historically accurate? Are those changes small and insignificant? Do those changes drastically differ from what we know to be accurate?

5. Why do you think the author alters the history?

6. Why do you think the author chose to write about this historical period?

CHAPTER 10

A Variety of Genres and Text Complexity

Read and comprehend complex literary and informational texts independently and proficiently (CCSS, p. 10).

What students need to . . .

KNOW

- Literary texts
- Informational texts

UNDERSTAND

- Literature encompasses a broad range of literary genres (e.g., stories, drama, poetry) that offer unique perspectives to readers.
- Informational texts provide readers with knowledge.

DO

- Read complex literary and informational texts independently and proficiently.
- Comprehend complex literary and informational texts independently and proficiently.

Pedagogical Foundations

CCR10 emphasizes the absolute necessity of students developing reading skills at higher levels than are currently being reported by multiple national sources, including private-sector and federal and state studies. Although it is important for students to find a genre with which they have an affinity, it is equally critical that they experiment with and gain an appreciation of multiple genres (Blachowicz & Ogle, 2008; Calkins, 1994; Duke, Caughlan, Juzwik, & Martin, 2012; Duke & Roberts, 2010; Gambrell, Malloy, & Mazzoni, 2011; Ogle & Blachowicz, 2002; Ranker, 2011; Smith, 1994). Similarly, allowing students to read at their independent reading level as a means of comfort and stability has real value to readers, especially struggling readers. Nonetheless, students must also be encouraged to push their skills to more advanced texts with appropriate scaffolding and interventions in place to ensure success (Biancarosa, 2012; Brabham & Villaume, 2002; Chauvin & Molina, 2012; Coleman, 2011; Fisher, Frey, & Lapp, 2012; Gewertz, 2013; Mesmer, Cunningham, & Hiebert, 2012; Shanahan, Fisher, & Frey, 2012). Taken together, this standard provides a significant foundation to move students forward in their overall reading experiences as well as in their development as learners and readers in a fast-developing technological world.

●●●●●●●●●●

Transitional Steps for Student Mastery

In kindergarten, students begin with group reading activities. Grade-one students should be reading prose, poetry, and age-appropriate informational text. Grade-two students are expected to read at the high end of the grades 2–3 text-complexity range, and in grade three drama is added. Grade-four students are expected to read at the grades 4–5 text complexity band with scaffolding as needed. This scaffolding is taken away in grade five with students expected to read at the high end of the complexity band independently and proficiently. Students in grades six and seven should be reading at the high end of the grades 6–8 complexity band with scaffolding as needed. They also begin reading literary nonfiction. Grade-eight students should read at the high end of this complexity independently and proficiently. Grade-nine students move to the high end of the grades 9–10 complexity band with scaffolding; grade-ten students read at the high end of the band independently and with proficiency. Grade-eleven students read in the high end of the grades 11–CCR text complexity band with scaffolding as needed. As with the previous grades, this scaffolding is removed in grade twelve with students expected to read independently and with proficiency at the high end of the range.

Text Complexity

The architects of Common Core State Standards fashioned CCR10 as the culmination of the previous nine standards. It builds on all of the other reading expectations and encompasses their skills in order to accomplish its goal of students reading across a wide range of genres and reading complexities. In effect, CCR10 collapses unless students experience rigorous instruction in CCR1–9. Of equal concern, however, remains the absolute necessity of exposing students to a diet of varied literary and informational text. To accomplish this, we need to address two questions: (1) What makes a text complex, and (2) how do we afford struggling students opportunities with these texts when they labor to make meaning from "easy" text? Because of the unique needs of Anchor Standard 10, the format of this chapter differs. Here, we analyze the true meaning of text complexity as well as offer scaffolding tips for greater range and text complexity.

Text complexity is a concept that many educators grapple with as they attempt to determine its influence in their instructional practice and as additional questions arise. What exactly does "complex" mean? How do we know if what students read rates as truly challenging? Can the same complex text be used for all our struggling students?

Let's begin with how we determine what makes a text complex. The Common Core State Standards Initiative suggests that these three factors constitute a rigorous text:

1. Quantitative aspects
2. Qualitative aspects
3. Matching the reader to both the text and the task assigned to it

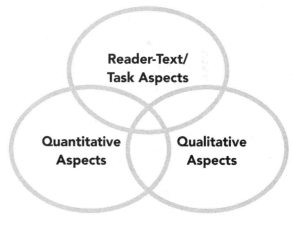

Quantitative evaluation of texts refers to those aspects of the text that you can count and express in numbers.

- Look at the words in the text themselves. Are they one-syllable words, or are they multisyllabic? Longer words suggest a text will be more difficult for readers to comprehend.

- Consider word frequency. Are the words common in everyday reading, or are they rare—perhaps more academic or domain-specific?

- Move on to the sentences. Are they short, or are they long and syntactically complex?

- Now review the text as a whole. How long is it? Brief texts typically require less cognitive resources for students to make meaning. In the case of struggling readers, the longer the text, the harder it is for them to keep their grasp of individual words as they work to comprehend longer passages.

Qualitative evaluation views the text through the lens of structure, language, and meaning.

- Can you identify the text structure? This is a significant aspect of the text; students who recognize the structure approach the reading differently because they are aware that the narrative or information will be presented in a unique way and are searching for signposts to guide their comprehension. Text structure also influences complexity, as it inherently alters the rigor of the content. For example, sequential passages follow a direct, easily observable flow of events or ideas—one after the other. Cause and effect, on the other hand, requires readers to differentiate between outcomes and causation with content that may not follow a linear progression, forcing students to classify content from throughout the text rather than in a chronological manner. In nonfiction text, specifically, text features expand the reading experience as they build a support system for accessing the content, but they require students to be familiar with them and how they function.

- Look at the text in a more global sense. Is the genre presenting the content in a simple or a sophisticated way? Does it demand domain-specific understanding?

- Examine the writing style of the author. Is it reader-friendly, or does it contain more sophisticated syntax?

- Look at the way the author uses language. Do you see examples of nonliteral language that fundamentally requires deeper understanding of vocabulary and how words and phrases are used?

- Survey the ideas and themes. Does the author describe them explicitly, or must readers draw conclusions and construct meaning independently?

The third factor shifts attention from the text to readers, centering on engagement. Think about these questions:

- Does the student have the background knowledge needed to access this text?
- Would this text interest or motivate the student to read?

Taken together, these factors present a framework to evaluate text complexity and determine how rigorous your expectations may be, taking into account the text and student. The next question is much more problematic: *How do we help struggling students access these texts with confidence and independence?*

Use the Text Complexity Checklist on the following page to determine the complexity of your texts and then make a decision as to their suitability for your students. Consider these questions: *Is the text too simple? Is it difficult? If so, will it become comprehensible to students with added support? Is the text so complex that students simply lack the resources to comprehend it?*

While the checklist will facilitate the selection of appropriate texts for your students, it's essential to expose them to a range of texts with varying levels of complexity. Thus, the last portion of this chapter offers 30 simple scaffolding tips to address Anchor Standard 10 and ensure that your students are on their way to becoming strong, independent readers and thinkers.

Targeted Reading Interventions for the Common Core © 2014 by Diana Sisson & Betsy Sisson, Scholastic Teaching Resources

Text Complexity Checklist

Use this checklist to determine text complexity.
Each item you check indicates an increase in the
rigor of the text.

QUANTITATIVE EVALUATION

- [ ] Multisyllabic words
- [ ] Rarely used words; words from the academic domain
- [ ] Lengthy sentences
- [ ] Lengthy text
- [ ] Nonlinear text structure

QUALITATIVE EVALUATION

- [ ] Presence of text features (e.g., diagrams, graphs, charts, icons, sidebars, and so on)
- [ ] Sophisticated genre
- [ ] Unusual writing style
- [ ] Complex sentences
- [ ] Nonliteral language
- [ ] Implicit ideas or themes

READER AND TASK EVALUATION

- [ ] Prior knowledge needed
- [ ] Student interest lacking
- [ ] Student motivation lacking

30 Scaffolding Tips to Promote Greater Range and Text Complexity

Challenging text is often an insurmountable hurdle for educators. How do you help students who struggle to access on-level text approach readings that may be challenging for students who don't struggle? We recommend a variety of instructional support techniques. Each of them affords students a different means to learn as readers as well as to experience text in unique ways . . . and they reflect our instructional drivers for student success!

1. **Nonfiction texts** should form nearly three-quarters of student reading with explicit instruction on how to approach this genre, such as its text structure and text features.

2. **Text features** offer inherent support systems within text. Students need only learn how to use them.

3. **A structured independent reading program** provides struggling students with the most powerful tool for strengthening their reading—time to practice and refine their skills.

4. **Assistive technology, such as text readers,** appeals to students' affinity for technology and commonly incorporates support tools such as dictionaries and highlighting features, thereby increasing engagement and motivation.

5. **Chunking text** is a hallmark for reading interventions as it allows students to focus on manageable pieces of text with greater possibilities for success.

6. **Written response to text** enables students to express their thinking in ways that allow them to be metacognitive and educators to assess their learning.

7. **Gradual increase of texts (both length and complexity)** improves comprehension in a measured, supportive environment.

8. **Build reading stamina** so that students have the mental fortitude to read challenging texts.

9. **Layered reading (preview, read, review)** functions as a means to chunk learning as well as to monitor understanding.

10. **Reading guides** focus student attention on key ideas of the text.

11. **Morphology (roots, prefixes, and suffixes) study** develops vocabulary skills, including in the academic domains, which frees cognitive resources at the word level to focus on passage comprehension.

12. **Marking up text with personal connections and related questions** encourages students to interact with the text as active learners.

13. **Genre studies** accord students the chance to read from a variety of genres with a clear focus on what makes each genre unique. This awareness of specific genres helps students understand how to approach texts from these genres, thus increasing their facility with and ultimately, their comprehension of them.

14. **Thematic units** allow students to explore varied genres and texts within an instructionally supported framework.

15. **Book clubs** afford student choices in a variety of texts with the added benefit of collaboration with classmates.

16. **Setting a purpose for reading** provides a mind-set for students as they begin the reading process and structures their attempts to make meaning throughout the text.

17. **Text structure analysis** furnishes students with a framework they can use to approach text.

18. **Pairing books with film** proves to be an inherently engaging activity with strong elements of visual support.

19. **Pairing fictional texts with nonfiction readings** expands the parameters of students' familiarity with varied genres and text.

20. **Explicit instruction in comprehension strategies** remains fundamental to supportive instruction for struggling readers.

21. **Television close captioning** offers a twist to reading supports as students can read along as they hear the words of the characters or narrator.

22. **Reading-writing connections** should be integral in all instructional activities, as reading and writing serve to strengthen each other. By writing, students can deepen their reflection on and understanding of readings. By reading, students improve their writing skills.

23. **Text-based questioning** requires students to refer back to the text and be responsive to its central message.

24. **Frontloading of text prior to reading** aids students when they are confronted by text they have no familiarity or experience with.

25. **Emphasizing varied reading techniques, such as skimming and scanning,** adds tools for struggling readers to utilize when working with rigorous text.

26. **Discourse style (e.g., humor, parody, satire),** not commonly read, demands that students have explicit instruction in order to understand how to approach it.

27. **Engaging students in analytical discussions of text** fosters their ability to dig deeply into a text in a collaborative environment with instructional support.

28. **Graphic organizers, aids, and representations** all operate as instructional supports of challenging texts, engaging students' senses as well as providing frameworks upon which to build understanding.

29. **Nonliteral language** abounds in upper elementary and middle school. Without direct instruction, students will flounder when confronted with metaphors, idioms, symbolism, and so on.

30. **Digital reading instruction** should be integrated into the reading program. The skills required for online readers differ widely from that of traditional print media.

Name _____ Date _____

DEVELOPING THEME

What theme is emerging? How is it affected by the characters? The setting? The plot?

What do you think the theme of this story is? Is it affected by the characters? The setting? The plot?

Middle

Beginning

- What are the characters doing?

- Where and when is the story set? How does the setting affect the story?

- What is happening in the plot? What action is taking place?

- What are the characters doing?

- Where and when is the story set? How does the setting affect the story?

- What is happening in the plot? What action is taking place?

- What are the characters doing?

- Where and when is the story set? How does the setting affect the story?

- What is happening in the plot? What action is taking place?

End

Has the theme changed in any way? Has it been affected by the characters? The setting? The plot?

Name _____ Date _____

BUILDING BLOCKS OF CENTRAL IDEA

What is the **topic**?
How does the main idea of this passage explain the topic?

What is the **main idea** of this passage?

What is the **detail** from this passage?	What is the **detail** from this passage?	What is the **detail** from this passage?

Don't forget: The individual details come together to form a central (main) idea, and central ideas tell the reader about the topic—creating building blocks of understanding!

Name _____ Date _____

4 Ws

WHEN	WHO	WHERE	WHAT
When does the information in the text take place? (If there is no specific time listed, continue to the next column.)	Who or what is the subject of the text?	Where does the information in the text take place? (If there is no specific location listed, continue to the next column.)	What did the subject do, or what happened to the subject?
→	→	→	

Use your 4 Ws to write a summary of the text.

Summary of _____:

Targeted Reading Interventions for the Common Core © 2014 by Diana Sisson & Betsy Sisson, Scholastic Teaching Resources

Name _____ Date _____

CHARACTER FRAME

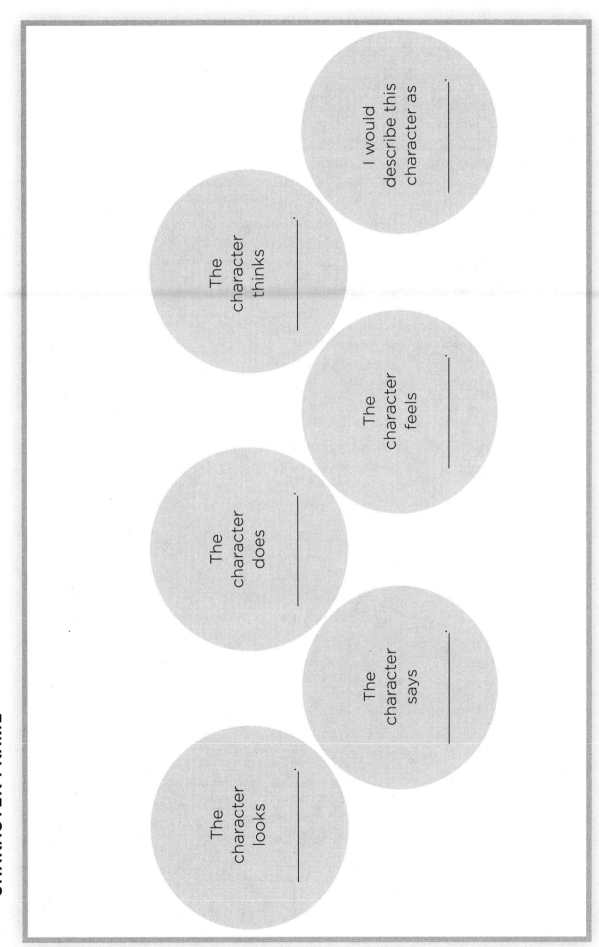

The character looks _____

The character does _____

The character thinks _____

The character feels _____

The character says _____

I would describe this character as _____

Name _____ Date _____

COMPARING AND CONTRASTING NARRATIVE ELEMENTS

Look at the details that you located.
How are they similar?

DETAILS

_____   _____

DETAILS

How do they differ?

Targeted Reading Interventions for the Common Core © 2014 by Diana Sisson & Betsy Sisson, Scholastic Teaching Resources

AUTHOR'S CHOICE SPINNER

Copy the spinner pattern and glue it to oak tag. Color with markers if you wish. Use scissors to punch a hole in the center of the spinner. Place a paper clip over the hole, as shown. Insert the brass fastener through the paper clip and hole. Spread the fastener tabs apart on the back of the spinner. Make sure the paper clip can spin freely.

Fastener

Solution

Character

Problem

Setting

Sequence
of Events

SIMILE POEM

Me!

My hair is as _____ as _____ .

My face is as _____ as _____ .

My eyes are as _____ as _____ .

My mouth is as _____ as _____ .

∿∿∿∿∿∿∿∿∿∿∿∿

My arms are as _____ as _____ .

My legs are as _____ as _____ .

My feet are as _____ as _____ .

∿∿∿∿∿∿∿∿∿∿∿∿

My brain is as _____ as _____ .

My heart is as _____ as _____ .

Put it all together, and you have ME!

Name _____ Date _____

WHAT DO I SEE AND HEAR?

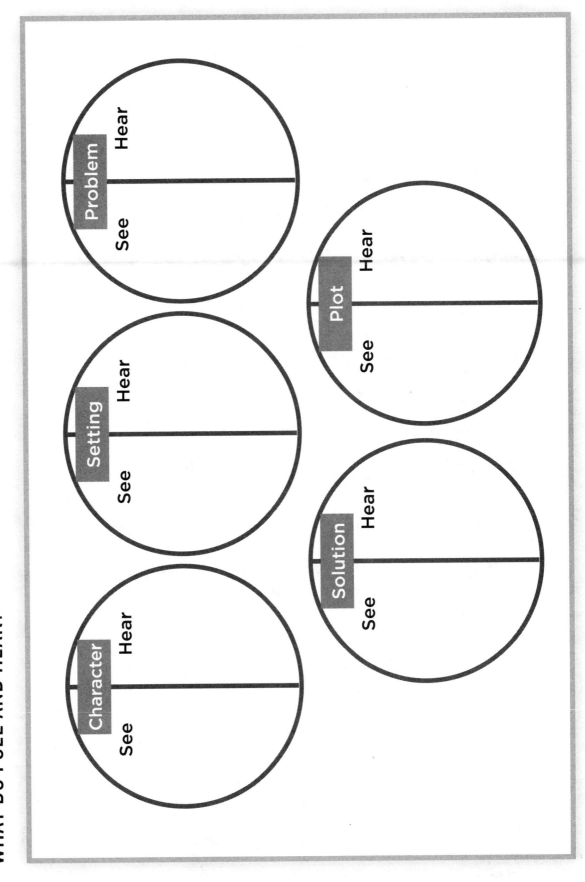

Name _____ Date _____

INSIDE POETRY

READING THE POEM	CHARACTERISTICS OF POETRY	LISTENING TO THE POEM
	Rhythm	
	Rhyme	
	Alliteration	
	Simile	
	Metaphor	
	Symbolism	
	Imagery	

Targeted Reading Interventions for the Common Core © 2014 by Diana Sisson & Betsy Sisson, Scholastic Teaching Resources

Name _____ Date _____

BOOK TO FILM

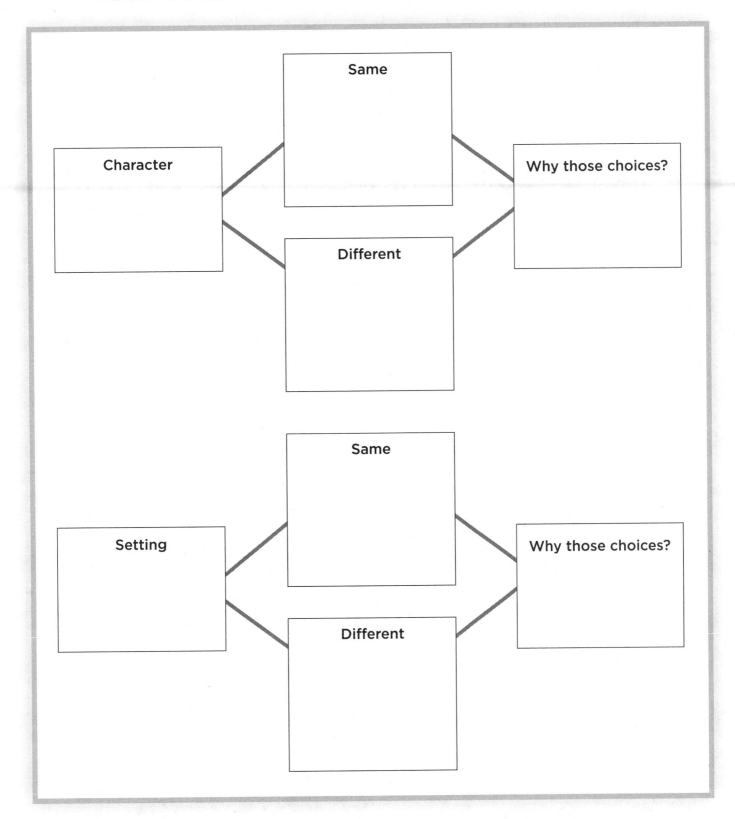

Name _____ Date _____

BOOK TO FILM *(CONTINUED)*

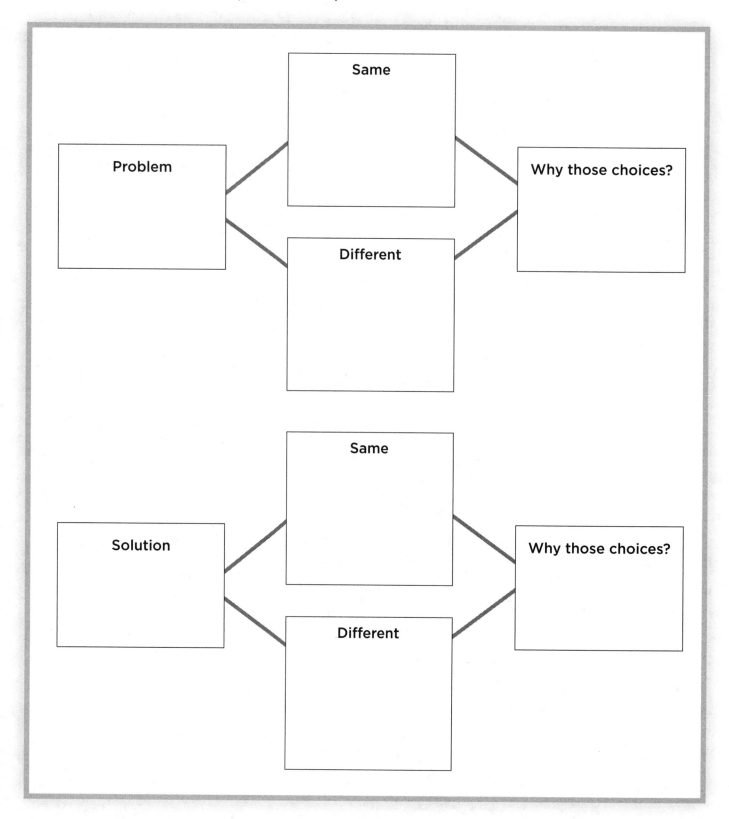

Targeted Reading Interventions for the Common Core © 2014 by Diana Sisson & Betsy Sisson, Scholastic Teaching Resources

Name _____ Date _____

SIDE-BY-SIDE MAPS

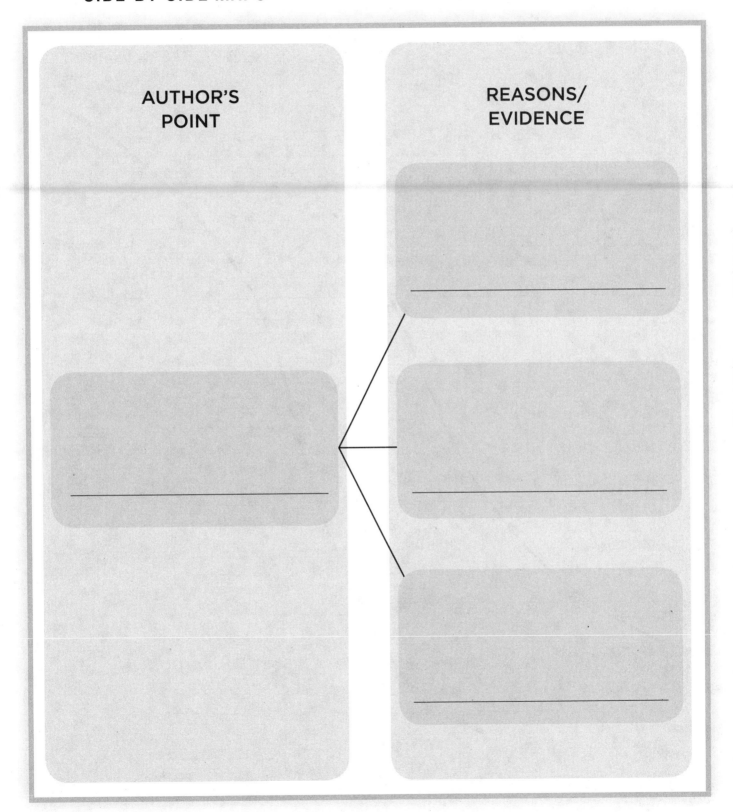

AUTHOR'S POINT

REASONS/ EVIDENCE

Name _____ Date _____

ARGUMENT PATHWAY

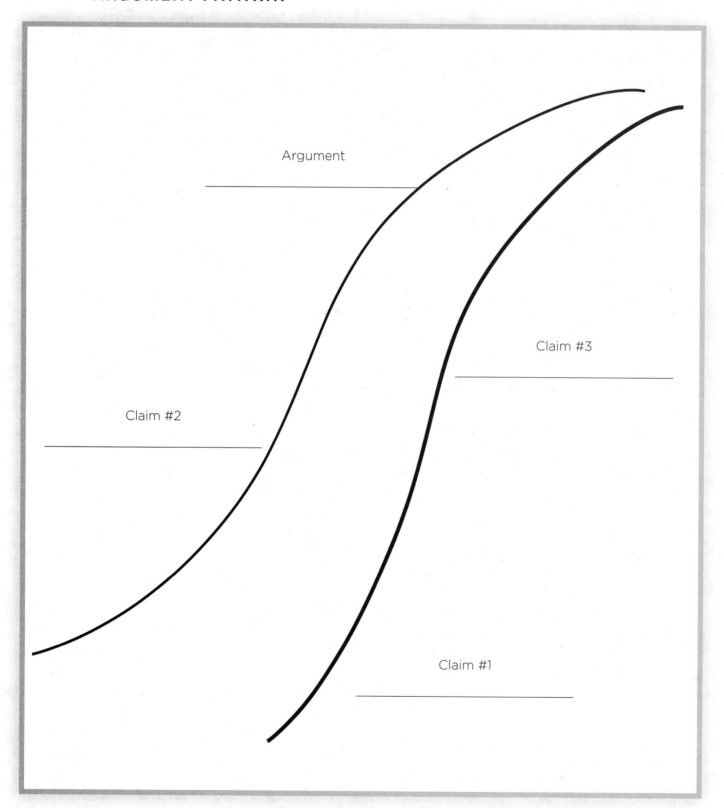

Argument

_____

Claim #3

_____

Claim #2

_____

Claim #1

_____

Name _____ Date _____

FACT OR OPINION?

ARGUMENT What is the argument in this text? _____ _____	FACT Can the author prove this statement?	OPINION Does the author share his or her thoughts or feelings? Can the author prove this statement?
Page #: _____ Evidence (a specific quote): _____ _____ Analyze the Evidence (How does this statement support the argument?): _____ _____		
Page #: _____ Evidence (a specific quote): _____ _____ Analyze the Evidence (How does this statement support the argument?): _____ _____		
Page #: _____ Evidence (a specific quote): _____ _____ Analyze the Evidence (How does this statement support the argument?): _____ _____		

Appendix A

COMMON CORE STATE STANDARDS FOR ENGLISH LANGUAGE ARTS & LITERACY IN HISTORY/SOCIAL STUDIES, SCIENCE, AND TECHNICAL SUBJECTS: AN OVERVIEW

What are the Common Core State Standards (CCSS)?

- Coordinated by the National Governors Association (NGA) and the Council of Chief State School Officers (CCSSO)
- Benchmarked with international standards
- Correlated with college and career expectations
- Aligned with NAEP Reading Framework
- Encompassing broad expectations that are cumulative and scaffolded for K–12 for both literary and nonfiction texts
- Sets grade-level expectations

What are the limitations of the Common Core State Standards?

- No prescription for how to teach
- No description of accelerated study
- No explanation of intervention supports
- No specialized plan for ELL or special needs students

What is the design of the CCSS?

- K–5 (cross-disciplinary)
- 6–12 English Language Arts
- 6–12 Literacy in History/Social Studies, Science, and Technical Subjects

COLLEGE AND CAREER READINESS
ANCHOR STANDARDS FOR READING

Key Ideas and Details

1. Read closely to determine what the text says explicitly and to make logical inferences from it; cite specific textual evidence when writing or speaking to support conclusions drawn from the text.

2. Determine central ideas or themes of a text and analyze their development; summarize the key supporting details and ideas.

3. Analyze how and why individuals, events, and ideas develop and interact over the course of a text.

Craft and Structure

4. Interpret words and phrases as they are used in a text, including determining technical, connotative, and figurative meanings, and analyze how specific word choices shape meaning or tone.

5. Analyze the structure of texts, including how specific sentences, paragraphs, and larger portions of the text (e.g., a section, chapter, scene, or stanza) relate to each other and the whole.

6. Assess how point of view or purpose shapes the content and style of a text.

Integration of Knowledge and Ideas

7. Integrate and evaluate content presented in diverse media and formats, including visually and quantitatively, as well as in words.

8. Delineate and evaluate the argument and specific claims in a text, including the validity of the reasoning as well as the relevance and sufficiency of the evidence.

9. Analyze how two or more texts address similar themes or topics in order to build knowledge or to compare the approaches the authors take.

Range of Reading and Level of Text Complexity

10. Read and comprehend complex literary and informational texts independently and proficiently.

Source: *http://www.corestandards.org/assets/CCSSI_ELA%20Standards.pdf*

STANDARDS FOR LITERATURE

STANDARD 1

Read closely to determine what the text says explicitly and to make logical inferences from it; cite specific textual evidence when writing or speaking to support conclusions drawn from the text.

Kindergarten	Grade 1	Grade 2
With prompting and support, ask and answer questions about key details in a text.	Ask and answer questions about key details in a text.	Ask and answer such questions as who, what, where, when, why, and how to demonstrate understanding of key details in a text.

Grade 3	Grade 4	Grade 5
Ask and answer questions to demonstrate understanding of a text, referring explicitly to the text as the basis for the answers.	Refer to details and examples in a text when explaining what the text says explicitly and when drawing inferences from the text.	Quote accurately from a text when explaining what the text says explicitly and when drawing inferences from the text.

Grade 6	Grade 7	Grade 8
Cite textual evidence to support analysis of what the text says explicitly as well as inferences drawn from the text.	Cite several pieces of textual evidence to support analysis of what the text says explicitly as well as inferences from the text.	Cite the textual evidence that most strongly supports an analysis of what the text says explicitly as well as inferences drawn from the text.

Grades 9–10		Grades 11–12	
Cite strong and thorough textual evidence to support analysis of what the text says explicitly as well as inferences drawn from the text.		Cite strong and thorough textual evidence to support analysis of what the text says explicitly as well as inferences drawn from the text, including determining where the text leaves matters uncertain.	

STANDARD 2

Determine central ideas or themes of a text and analyze their development; summarize the key supporting details and ideas.

Kindergarten	Grade 1	Grade 2
With prompting and support, retell familiar stories, including key details.	Retell stories, including key details, and demonstrate understanding of their central message or lesson.	Recount stories, including fables and folktales from diverse cultures, and determine their central message, lesson, or moral.

Grade 3	Grade 4	Grade 5
Recount stories, including fables, folktales, and myths from diverse cultures; determine the central message, lesson, or moral and explain how it is conveyed through key details in the text.	Determine the theme of a story, drama, or poem from details in the text; summarize the text.	Determine a theme of a story, drama, or poem from details in the text, including how characters in a story or drama respond to challenges or how the speaker in a poem reflects upon a topic; summarize the text.

Grade 6	Grade 7	Grade 8
Determine a theme or central idea of a text and how it is conveyed through particular details; provide a summary of the text distinct from personal opinions or judgments.	Determine a theme or central idea of a text and analyze its development over the course of the text; provide an objective summary of the text.	Determine a theme or central idea of a text and analyze its development over the course of the text, including its relationship to the characters, setting, and plot; provide an objective summary of the text.

Grades 9–10		Grades 11–12	
Determine a theme or central idea of a text and analyze in detail its development over the course of the text, including how it emerges and is shaped and refined by specific details; provide an objective summary of the text.		Determine two or more themes or central ideas of a text and analyze their development over the course of the text, including how they interact and build on one another to produce a complex account; provide an objective summary of the text.	

Targeted Reading Interventions for the Common Core © 2014 by Diana Sisson & Betsy Sisson, Scholastic Teaching Resources

STANDARD 3

Analyze how and why individuals, events, and ideas develop and interact over the course of a text.

Kindergarten	Grade 1	Grade 2
With prompting and support, identify characters, settings, and major events in a story.	Describe characters, settings, and major events in a story, using key details.	Describe how characters in a story respond to major events and challenges.

Grade 3	Grade 4	Grade 5
Describe characters in a story (e.g., their traits, motivations, or feelings) and explain how their actions contribute to the sequence of events.	Describe in depth a character, setting, or event in a story or drama, drawing on specific details in the text (e.g., a character's thoughts, words or actions).	Compare and contrast two or more characters, settings, or events in a story or drama, drawing on specific details in the text (e.g., how characters interact).

Grade 6	Grade 7	Grade 8
Describe how a particular story's or drama's plot unfolds in a series of episodes as well as how the characters respond or change as the plot moves toward a resolution.	Analyze how particular elements of a story or drama interact (e.g., how setting shapes the characters or plot).	Analyze how particular lines of dialogue or incidents in a story or drama propel the action, reveal aspects of a character, or provoke a decision.

Grades 9–10	Grades 11–12
Analyze how complex characters (e.g., those with multiple or conflicting motivations) develop over the course of a text, interact with other characters, and advance the plot or develop the theme.	Analyze the impact of the author's choices regarding how to develop and relate elements of a story or drama (e.g., where a story is set, how the action is ordered, how the characters are introduced and developed).

STANDARD 4

Interpret words and phrases as they are used in a text, including determining technical, connotative, and figurative meanings, and analyze how specific word choices shape meaning or tone.

Kindergarten	Grade 1	Grade 2
Ask and answer questions about unknown words in a text.	Identify words and phrases in stories or poems that suggest feelings or appeal to the senses.	Describe how words and phrases (e.g., regular beats, alliteration, rhymes, repeated lines) supply rhythm and meaning in a story, poem, or song.

Grade 3	Grade 4	Grade 5
Determine the meaning of words and phrases as they are used in a text, distinguishing literal from nonliteral language.	Determine the meaning of words and phrases as they are used in a text, including those that allude to significant characters found in mythology (e.g., Herculean).	Determine the meaning of words and phrases as they are used in a text, including figurative language such as metaphors and similes.

Grade 6	Grade 7	Grade 8
Determine the meaning of words and phrases as they are used in a text, including figurative and connotative meanings; analyze the impact of a specific word choice on meaning and tone.	Determine the meaning of words and phrases as they are used in a text, including figurative and connotative meanings; analyze the impact of rhymes and other repetitions of sounds (e.g., alliteration) on a specific verse or stanza of a poem or section of a story or drama.	Determine the meaning of words and phrases as they are used in a text, including figurative and connotative meanings; analyze the impact of specific word choices on meaning and tone, including analogies or allusions to other texts.

Grades 9–10	Grades 11–12
Determine the meaning of words and phrases as they are used in the text, including figurative and connotative meanings; analyze the cumulative impact of specific word choices on meaning and tone (e.g., how the language evokes a sense of time and place; how it sets a formal or informal tone).	Determine the meaning of words and phrases as they are used in the text, including figurative and connotative meanings; analyze the impact of specific word choices on meaning and tone, including words with multiple meanings or language that is particularly fresh, engaging, or beautiful. (Include Shakespeare as well as other authors).

STANDARD 5

Analyze the structure of texts, including how specific sentences, paragraphs, and larger portions of the text (e.g., a section, chapter, scene, or stanza) relate to each other and the whole.

Kindergarten	Grade 1	Grade 2
Recognize common types of texts (e.g., storybooks, poems).	Explain major differences between books that tell stories and books that give information, drawing on a wide range or text types.	Describe the overall structure of a story, including describing how the beginning introduces the story and the ending concludes the action.

Grade 3	Grade 4	Grade 5
Refer to parts of stories, dramas, and poems when writing or speaking about a text, using terms such as chapter, scene, and stanza; describe how each successive part builds on earlier sections.	Explain major differences between poems, drama, and prose, and refer to the structural elements of poems (e.g., verse, rhythm, meter) and drama (e.g., casts of characters, settings, descriptions, dialogue, stage directions) when writing or speaking about a text.	Explain how a series of chapters, scenes, or stanzas fit together to provide the overall structure of a particular story, drama, or poem.

Grade 6	Grade 7	Grade 8
Analyze how a particular sentence, chapter, scene, or stanza fits into the overall structure of a text and contributes to the development of theme, setting, or plot.	Analyze how a drama's or poem's form or structure (e.g., soliloquy, sonnet) contributes to its meaning.	Compare and contrast the structure of two or more texts and analyze how the differing structure of each text contributes to its meaning and style.

Grades 9–10	Grades 11–12
Analyze how an author's choices concerning how to structure a text, order events within it (e.g., parallel plots) and manipulate time (e.g., pacing, flashbacks) create such effects as mystery, tension, or surprise.	Analyze how an author's choices concerning how to structure specific parts of a text (e.g., the choice of where to begin or end a story, the choice to provide a comedic or tragic resolution) contribute to its overall structure and meaning as well as its aesthetic impact.

STANDARD 6

Assess how point of view or purpose shapes the content and style of a text.

Kindergarten	Grade 1	Grade 2
With prompting and support, name the author and illustrator of a story and define the role of each in telling the story.	Identify who is telling the story at various points in a text.	Acknowledge differences in the points of view of characters, including by speaking in a different voice for each character when reading dialogue aloud.

Grade 3	Grade 4	Grade 5
Distinguish their own point of view from that of the narrator or those of the characters.	Compare and contrast the point of view from which different stories are narrated, including the difference between first- and third-person narrations.	Describe how a narrator's or speaker's point of view influences how events are described.

Grade 6	Grade 7	Grade 8
Explain how an author develops the point of view of the narrator or speaker in a text.	Analyze how an author develops and contrasts the points of view of different characters or narrators in a text.	Analyze how differences in the points of view of the characters and the audience or reader (e.g., created through the use of dramatic irony) create such effects as suspense or humor.

Grades 9–10	Grades 11–12
Analyze a particular point of view or cultural experience reflected in a work of literature from outside the United States, drawing on a wide reading of world literature.	Analyze a case in which grasping point of view requires distinguishing what is directly stated in a text from what is really meant (e.g., satire, sarcasm, irony, or understatement).

STANDARD 7

Integrate and evaluate content presented in diverse media and formats, including visually and quantitatively, as well as in words.

Kindergarten	Grade 1	Grade 2
With prompting and support, describe the relationship between illustrations and the story in which they appear (e.g., what moment in a story an illustration depicts).	Use illustrations and details in a story to describe its characters, setting, or events.	Use information gained from the illustrations and words in a print or digital text to demonstrate understanding of its characters, setting, or plot.

Grade 3	Grade 4	Grade 5
Explain how specific aspects of a text's illustrations contribute to what is conveyed by the words in a story (e.g., create mood, emphasize aspects of a character or setting).	Make connections between the text of a story or drama and a visual or oral presentation of the text, identifying where each version reflects specific descriptions and directions in the text.	Analyze how visual and multimedia elements contribute to the meaning, tone, or beauty of a text (e.g., graphic novel, multimedia presentation of fiction, folktale, myth, poem).

Grade 6	Grade 7	Grade 8
Compare and contrast the experience of reading a story, drama, or poem to listening to or viewing an audio, video, or live version of the text, including contrasting what they "see" and "hear" when reading the text to what they perceive when they listen or watch.	Compare and contrast a written story, drama, or poem to its audio, filmed, staged, or multimedia version, analyzing the effects of techniques unique to each medium (e.g., lighting, sound, color, or camera focus and angles in a film).	Analyze the extent to which a filmed or live production of a story or drama stays faithful to or departs from the text or script, evaluating the choices made by the director or actors.

Grades 9–10	Grades 11–12
Analyze the representation of a subject or a key scene in two different artistic mediums, including what is emphasized or absent in each treatment (e.g., Auden's "Musée des Beaux Arts" and Breughel's *Landscape with the Fall of Icarus*).	Analyze multiple interpretations of a story, drama, or poem (e.g., recorded or live production of a play or recorded novel or poetry), evaluating how each version interprets the source text. (Include at least one play by Shakespeare and one play by an American dramatist.)

STANDARD 8

Delineate and evaluate the argument and specific claims in a text, including the validity of the reasoning as well as the relevance and sufficiency of the evidence.

Not applicable to literature

STANDARD 9

Analyze how two or more texts address similar themes or topics in order to build knowledge or to compare the approaches the authors take.

Kindergarten	Grade 1	Grade 2
With prompting and support, compare and contrast the adventures and experiences of characters in familiar stories.	Compare and contrast the adventures and experiences of characters in stories.	Compare and contrast two or more versions of the same story (e.g., Cinderella stories) by different authors or from different cultures.

Grade 3	Grade 4	Grade 5
Compare and contrast the themes, settings, and plots of stories written by the same author about the same or similar characters (e.g., in books from a series).	Compare and contrast the treatment of similar themes and topics (e.g., opposition of good and evil) and patterns of events (e.g., the quest) in stories, myths, and traditional literature from different cultures.	Compare and contrast stories in the same genre (e.g., mysteries and adventure stories) on their approaches to similar themes and topics.

Grade 6	Grade 7	Grade 8
Compare and contrast texts in different forms or genres (e.g., stories and poems, historical novels and fantasy stories) in terms of their approaches to similar themes and topics.	Compare and contrast a fictional portrayal of a time, place, or character, and a historical account of the same period as a means of understanding how authors of fiction use or alter history.	Analyze how a modern work of fiction draws on themes, patterns of events, or character types from myths, traditional stories, or religious works such as the Bible, including describing how the material is rendered new.

Grades 9–10	Grades 11–12
Analyze how an author draws on and transforms source materials in a specific work (e.g., how Shakespeare treats a theme or topic from Ovid or the Bible or how a later author draws on a play by Shakespeare).	Demonstrate knowledge of eighteenth-, nineteenth-, and early-twentieth-century foundational works of American literature, including how two or more texts from the same period treat similar themes or topics.

STANDARD 10

Read and comprehend complex literary and informational texts independently and proficiently.

Kindergarten	Grade 1	Grade 2
Actively engage in group reading activities with purpose and understanding.	With prompting and support, read prose and poetry of appropriate complexity for grade 1.	By the end of the year, read and comprehend literature, including stories and poetry, in the grades 2-3 complexity band proficiently, with scaffolding as needed at the high end of the range.

Grade 3	Grade 4	Grade 5
By the end of the year, read and comprehend literature, including stories, dramas, and poetry at the high end of the grades 2–3 complexity band independently and proficiently.	By the end of the year, read and comprehend literature, including stories, dramas, and poetry, in the grades 4–5 complexity band proficiently, with scaffolding as needed at the high end of the range.	By the end of the year, read and comprehend literature, including stories, drama, and poetry, at the high end of the grades 4–5 complexity band independently and proficiently.

Grade 6	Grade 7	Grade 8
By the end of the year, read and comprehend literature, including stories, dramas, and poems, in the grades 6–8 complexity band proficiently, with scaffolding as needed at the high end of the range.	By the end of the year, read and comprehend literature, including stories, dramas, and poems, in the grades 6–8 complexity band proficiently, with scaffolding as needed at the high end of the range.	By the end of the year, read and comprehend literature, including stories, dramas, and poems, at the high end of the grades 6–8 complexity bank independently and proficiently.

Grades 9–10	Grades 11–12
By the end of grade 9, read and comprehend literature, including stories, dramas, and poems, in the grades 9–10 text complexity band proficiently, with scaffolding as needed at the high end of the range. By the end of grade 10, read and comprehend literature, including stories, dramas, and poems, at the high end of the grades 9–10 text complexity band independently and proficiently.	By the end of grade 11, read and comprehend literature, including stories, dramas, or poems, in the grades 11-CCR text complexity band proficiently, with scaffolding as needed at the high end of the range. By the end of grade 12, read and comprehend literature, including stories, dramas, and poems, at the high end of the grades 11-CCR text complexity band independently and proficiently.

Source: *http://www.corestandards.org/assets/CCSSI_ELA%20Standards.pdf*

STANDARDS FOR INFORMATIONAL TEXT

STANDARD 1

Read closely to determine what the text says explicitly and to make logical inferences from it; cite specific textual evidence when writing or speaking to support conclusions drawn from the text.

Kindergarten	Grade 1	Grade 2
With prompting and support, ask and answer questions about key details in a text.	Ask and answer questions about key details in a text.	Ask and answer such questions as who, what, where, when, why, and how to demonstrate understanding of key details in a text.

Grade 3	Grade 4	Grade 5
Ask and answer questions to demonstrate understanding of a text, referring explicitly to the text as the basis for the answers.	Refer to details and examples in a text when explaining what the text says explicitly and when drawing inferences from the text.	Quote accurately from a text when explaining what the text says explicitly and when drawing inferences from the text.

Grade 6	Grade 7	Grade 8
Cite textual evidence to support analysis of what the text says explicitly as well as inferences drawn from the text.	Cite several pieces of textual evidence to support analysis of what the text says explicitly as well as inferences drawn from the text.	Cite the textual evidence that most strongly supports an analysis of what the text says explicitly as well as inferences drawn from the text.

Grades 9–10	Grades 11–12
Cite strong and thorough textual evidence to support analysis of what the text says explicitly as well as inferences drawn from the text.	Cite strong and thorough textual evidence to support analysis of what the text says explicitly as well as inferences drawn from the text, including determining where the text leaves matters uncertain.

STANDARD 2

Determine central ideas or themes of a text and analyze their development; summarize the key supporting details and ideas.

Kindergarten	Grade 1	Grade 2
With prompting and support, identify the main topic and retell key details of a text.	Identify the main topic and retell key details of a text.	Identify the main topic of a multiparagraph text as well as the focus of specific paragraphs within the text.

Grade 3	Grade 4	Grade 5
Determine the main idea of a text; recount the key details and explain how they support the main idea.	Determine the main idea of a text and explain how it is supported by key details; summarize the text.	Determine two or more main ideas of a text and explain how they are supported by key details; summarize the text.

Grade 6	Grade 7	Grade 8
Determine a central idea of a text and how it is conveyed through particular details; provide a summary of the text distinct from personal opinions or judgments.	Determine two or more central ideas in a text and analyze their development over the course of the text; provide an objective summary of the text.	Determine a central idea of a text and analyze its development over the course of the text, including its relationship to supporting ideas; provide an objective summary of the text.

Grades 9–10	Grades 11–12
Determine a central idea of a text and analyze its development over the course of the text, including how it emerges and is shaped and refined by specific details; provide an objective summary of the text.	Determine two or more central ideas of a text and analyze their development over the course of the text, including how they interact and build on one another to provide a complex analysis; provide an objective summary of the text.

STANDARD 3

Analyze how and why individuals, events, and ideas develop and interact over the course of a text.

Kindergarten	Grade 1	Grade 2
With prompting and support, describe the connection between two individuals, events, ideas, or pieces of information in a text.	Describe the connection between two individuals, events, ideas, or pieces of information in a text.	Describe the connection between a series of historical events, scientific ideas or concepts, or steps in technical procedures in a text.

Grade 3	Grade 4	Grade 5
Describe the relationship between a series of historical events, scientific ideas or concepts, or steps in technical procedures in a text, using language that pertains to time, sequence, and cause/effect.	Explain events, procedures, ideas, or concepts in a historical, scientific, or technical text, including what happened and why, based on specific information in the text.	Explain the relationships or interactions between two or more individuals, events, ideas, or concepts in a historical, scientific, or technical text based on specific information in the text.

Grade 6	Grade 7	Grade 8
Analyze in detail how a key individual, event, or idea is introduced, illustrated, and elaborated in a text (e.g., through examples or anecdotes).	Analyze the interactions between individuals, events, and ideas in a text (e.g., how ideas influence individuals or events, or how individuals influence ideas or events).	Analyze how a text makes connections among and distinctions between individuals, ideas, or events (e.g., through comparisons, analogies, or categories).

Grades 9–10	Grades 11–12
Analyze how the author unfolds an analysis or series of ideas or events, including the order in which the points are made, how they are introduced and developed, and the connections that are drawn between them.	Analyze a complex set of ideas or sequence of events and explain how specific individuals, ideas, or events interact and develop over the course of the text.

STANDARD 4

Interpret words and phrases as they are used in a text, including determining technical, connotative, and figurative meanings, and analyze how specific word choices shape meaning or tone.

Kindergarten	Grade 1	Grade 2
With prompting and support, ask and answer questions about unknown words in a text.	Ask and answer questions to help determine or clarify the meaning of words and phrases in a text.	Determine the meaning of words and phrases in a text relevant to a grade 2 topic or subject area.

Grade 3	Grade 4	Grade 5
Determine the meaning of general academic and domain-specific words and phrases in a text relevant to a grade 3 topic or subject area.	Determine the meaning of general academic and domain-specific words or phrases in a text relevant to a grade 4 topic or subject area.	Determine the meaning of general academic and domain-specific words and phrases in a text relevant to a grade 5 topic or subject area.

Grade 6	Grade 7	Grade 8
Determine the meaning of words and phrases as they are used in a text, including figurative, connotative, and technical meanings.	Determine the meaning of words and phrases as they are used in a text, including figurative, connotative, and technical meanings; analyze the impact of a specific word choice on meaning and tone.	Determine the meaning of words and phrases as they are used in a text, including figurative, connotative, and technical meanings; analyze the impact of specific word choices on meaning and tone, including analogies or allusions to other texts.

Grades 9–10	Grades 11–12
Determine the meaning of words and phrases as they are used in a text, including figurative, connotative, and technical meanings; analyze the cumulative impact of specific word choices on meaning and tone (e.g., how the language of a court opinion differs from that of a newspaper).	Determine the meaning of words and phrases as they are used in a text, including figurative, connotative, and technical meanings; analyze how an author uses and refines the meaning of a key term or terms over the course of a text (e.g., how Madison defines *faction* in *Federalist* No. 10).

STANDARD 5

Analyze the structure of texts, including how specific sentences, paragraphs, and larger portions of the text (e.g., a section, chapter, scene, or stanza) relate to each other and the whole.

Kindergarten	Grade 1	Grade 2
Identify the front cover, back cover, and title page of a book.	Know and use various text features (e.g., headings, tables of contents, glossaries, electronic menus, icons) to locate key facts or information in a text.	Know and use various text features (e.g., captions, bold print, subheadings, glossaries, indexes, electronic menus, icons) to locate key facts or information in a text efficiently.

Grade 3	Grade 4	Grade 5
Use text features and search tools (e.g., key words, sidebars, hyperlinks) to locate information relevant to a given topic efficiently.	Describe the overall structure (e.g., chronology, comparison, cause/effect, problem/solution) of events, ideas, concepts, or information in a text or part of a text.	Compare and contrast the overall structure (e.g., chronology, comparison, cause/effect, problem/solution) of events, ideas, concepts, or information in two or more texts.

Grade 6	Grade 7	Grade 8
Analyze how a particular sentence, paragraph, chapter, or section fits into the overall structure of a text and contributes to the development of the ideas.	Analyze the structure an author uses to organize a text, including how the major sections contribute to the whole and to the development of the ideas.	Analyze in detail the structure of a specific paragraph in a text, including the role of particular sentences in developing and refining a key concept.

Grades 9–10	Grades 11–12
Analyze in detail how an author's ideas or claims are developed and refined by particular sentences, paragraphs, or larger portions of a text (e.g., a section or chapter).	Analyze and evaluate the effectiveness of the structure an author uses in his or her exposition or argument, including whether the structure makes points clear, convincing, and engaging.

STANDARD 6

Assess how point of view or purpose shapes the content and style of a text.

Kindergarten	Grade 1	Grade 2
Name the author and illustrator of a text and define the role of each in presenting the ideas or information in a text.	Distinguish between information provided by pictures or other illustrations and information provided by the words in a text.	Identify the main purpose of a text, including what the author wants to answer, explain, or describe.

Grade 3	Grade 4	Grade 5
Distinguish their own point of view from that of the author of a text.	Compare and contrast a firsthand and secondhand account of the same event or topic; describe the differences in focus and the information provided.	Analyze multiple accounts of the same event or topic, noting important similarities and differences in the point of view they represent.

Grade 6	Grade 7	Grade 8
Determine an author's point of view or purpose in a text and explain how it is conveyed in the text.	Determine an author's point of view or purpose in a text and analyze how the author distinguishes his or her position from that of others.	Determine an author's point of view or purpose in a text and analyze how the author acknowledges and responds to conflicting evidence or viewpoints.

Grades 9–10	Grades 11–12
Determine an author's point of view or purpose in a text and analyze how an author uses rhetoric to advance that point of view or purpose.	Determine an author's point of view or purpose in a text in which the rhetoric is particularly effective, analyzing how style and content contribute to the power, persuasiveness or beauty of the text.

STANDARD 7

Assess how point of view or purpose shapes the content and style of a text.

Kindergarten	Grade 1	Grade 2
With prompting and support, describe the relationship between illustrations and the text in which they appear (e.g., what person, place, thing, or idea in the text an illustration depicts).	Use the illustrations and details in a text to describe its key ideas.	Explain how specific images (e.g., a diagram showing how a machine works) contribute to and clarify a text.

Grade 3	Grade 4	Grade 5
Use information gained from illustrations (e.g., maps, photographs) and the words in a text to demonstrate understanding of the text (e.g., where, when, why, and how key events occur).	Interpret information presented visually, orally, or quantitatively (e.g., in charts, graphs, diagrams, time lines, animations, or interactive elements on Web pages) and explain how the information contributes to an understanding of the text in which it appears.	Draw on information from multiple print or digital sources, demonstrating the ability to locate an answer to a question quickly or to solve a problem efficiently.

Grade 6	Grade 7	Grade 8
Integrate information presented in different media or formats (e.g., visually, quantitatively) as well as in words to develop a coherent understanding of a topic or issue.	Compare and contrast a text to an audio, video, or multimedia version of the text, analyzing each medium's portrayal of the subject (e.g., how the delivery of a speech affects the impact of the words).	Evaluate the advantages and disadvantages of using different mediums (e.g., print or digital text, video, multimedia) to present a particular topic or idea.

Grades 9–10	Grades 11–12
Analyze various accounts of a subject told in different mediums (e.g., a person's life story in both print and multimedia), determining which details are emphasized in each account.	Integrate and evaluate multiple sources of information presented in different media or formats (e.g., visually, quantitatively) as well as in words in order to address a question or solve a problem.

STANDARD 8

Delineate and evaluate the argument and specific claims in a text, including the validity of the reasoning as well as the relevance and sufficiency of the evidence.

Kindergarten	Grade 1	Grade 2
With prompting and support, identify the reasons an author gives to support points in a text.	Identify the reasons an author gives to support points in a text.	Describe how reasons support specific points the author makes in a text.

Grade 3	Grade 4	Grade 5
Describe the logical connection between particular sentences and paragraphs in a text (e.g., comparison, cause/effect, first/second/third in a sequence).	Explain how an author uses reasons and evidence to support particular points in a text.	Explain how an author uses reasons and evidence to support particular points in a text, identifying which reasons and evidence support which point(s).

Grade 6	Grade 7	Grade 8
Trace and evaluate the argument and specific claims in a text, distinguishing claims that are supported by reasons and evidence from claims that are not.	Trace and evaluate the argument and specific claims in a text, assessing whether the reasoning is sound and the evidence is relevant and sufficient to support the claims.	Delineate and evaluate the argument and specific claims in a text, assessing whether the reasoning is sound and the evidence is relevant and sufficient; recognize when irrelevant evidence is introduced.

Grades 9–10	Grades 11–12
Delineate and evaluate the argument and specific claims in a text, assessing whether the reasoning is valid and the evidence is relevant and sufficient; identify false statements and fallacious reasoning.	Delineate and evaluate the reasoning in seminal U.S. texts, including the application of constitutional principles and use of legal reasoning (e.g., in U.S. Supreme Court majority opinions and dissents) and the premises, purposes, and arguments in works of public advocacy (e.g., *The Federalist*, presidential addresses).

Targeted Reading Interventions for the Common Core © 2014 by Diana Sisson & Betsy Sisson, Scholastic Teaching Resources

STANDARD 9

Analyze how two or more texts address similar themes or topics in order to build knowledge or to compare the approaches the authors take.

Kindergarten	Grade 1	Grade 2
With prompting and support, identify basic similarities in and differences between two texts on the same topic (e.g., in illustrations, descriptions, or procedures).	Identify basic similarities in and differences between two texts on the same topic (e.g., in illustrations, descriptions, or procedures).	Compare and contrast the most important points presented by two texts on the same topic.
Grade 3	**Grade 4**	**Grade 5**
Compare and contrast the most important points and key details presented in two texts on the same topic.	Integrate information from two texts on the same topic in order to write or speak about the subject knowledgeably.	Integrate information from several texts on the same topic in order to write or speak about the subject knowledgeably.
Grade 6	**Grade 7**	**Grade 8**
Compare and contrast one author's presentation of events with that of another (e.g., a memoir written by and a biography on the same person).	Analyze how two or more authors writing about the same topic shape their presentations of key information by emphasizing different evidence or advancing different interpretations of facts.	Analyze a case in which two or more texts provide conflicting information on the same topic and identify where the texts disagree on matters of fact or interpretation.

Grades 9–10	Grades 11–12
Analyze seminal U.S. documents of historical and literary significance (e.g., Washington's Farewell Address, the Gettysburg Address, Roosevelt's Four Freedoms speech, King's "Letter from Birmingham Jail"), including how they address related themes and concepts.	Analyze seventeenth-, eighteenth-, and nineteenth-century foundational U.S. documents of historical and literary significance (including The Declaration of Independence, the Preamble to the Constitution, the Bill of Rights, and Lincoln's Second Inaugural Address) for their themes, purposes, and rhetorical features.

STANDARD 10

Read and comprehend complex literary and informational texts independently and proficiently.

Kindergarten	Grade 1	Grade 2
Actively engage in group reading activities with purpose and understanding.	With prompting and support, read informational texts appropriately complex for grade 1.	By the end of year, read and comprehend informational texts, including history/social studies, science, and technical texts, in the grades 2–3 text complexity band proficiently, with scaffolding as needed at the high end of the range.
Grade 3	**Grade 4**	**Grade 5**
By the end of the year, read and comprehend informational texts, including history/social studies, science, and technical texts, at the high end of the grades 2–3 text complexity band independently and proficiently.	By the end of year, read and comprehend informational texts, including history/social studies, science, and technical texts, in the grades 4–5 text complexity band proficiently, with scaffolding as needed at the high end of the range.	By the end of the year, read and comprehend informational texts, including history/social studies, science, and technical texts, at the high end of the grades 4–5 text complexity band independently and proficiently.
Grade 6	**Grade 7**	**Grade 8**
By the end of the year, read and comprehend literary nonfiction in the grades 6–8 text complexity band proficiently, with scaffolding as needed at the high end of the range.	By the end of the year, read and comprehend literary nonfiction in the grades 6–8 text complexity band proficiently, with scaffolding as needed at the high end of the range.	By the end of the year, read and comprehend literary nonfiction at the high end of the grades 6–8 text complexity band independently and proficiently.

Grades 9–10	Grades 11–12
By the end of grade 9, read and comprehend literary nonfiction in the grades 9–10 text complexity band proficiently, with scaffolding as needed at the high end of the range. By the end of grade 10, read and comprehend literary nonfiction at the high end of the grades 9–10 text complexity band independently and proficiently.	By the end of grade 11, read and comprehend literary nonfiction in the grades 11-CCR text complexity band proficiently, with scaffolding as needed at the high end of the range. By the end of grade 12, read and comprehend literary nonfiction at the high end of the grades 11-CCR text complexity band independently and proficiently.

Source: *http://www.corestandards.org/assets/CCSSI_ELA%20Standards.pdf*

COLLEGE AND CAREER READINESS STANDARDS IN A NUTSHELL

	STANDARD	BIG IDEA
Key Ideas and Details	CCR Standard 1	*Reading for Details Using Both Literal and Inferential Understanding*
	CCR Standard 2	*Theme/Main Idea and Summarization*
	CCR Standard 3	*Narrative Elements (Character, Setting, Plot) and Sequence of Events*
Craft and Structure	CCR Standard 4	*Vocabulary in Context*
	CCR Standard 5	*Text Structure*
	CCR Standard 6	*Point of View and Author's Purpose*
Integration of Knowledge and Ideas	CCR Standard 7	*Diverse Text Formats and Media*
	CCR Standard 8	*Evaluate Arguments in Nonfiction Text (Not applicable to literature)*
	CCR Standard 9	*Comparing and Contrasting Multiple Texts*
Range of Reading and Level of Text Complexity	CCR Standard 10	*A Variety of Genres and Text Complexity*

KUDOs: An Overview

What Are KUDOs?

K   What do students need to **know**?

U   What do students need to **understand**?

DO   What do students need to **do**?

Breaking Down KUDOs: An Introduction

Use the KUDOs framework as a continuum of student learning. As an essential component of differentiated instruction, KUDOs provide a powerful method for educators to deconstruct the anchor standards into distinct, manageable, progressive chunks. KUDOs' progressive acquisition of learning is highlighted by its alignment to Bloom's Taxonomy (1956), which illustrates how learning gradually gains in cognitive rigor and application. Taken as a whole, KUDOs aid in planning for RtI interventions and delivering prescriptive, scaffolded teaching to meet the unique needs of all students.

Using KUDOs as a framework, educators first consider what factual knowledge students must KNOW in order to build their abilities within that anchor standard. This first piece of the framework is critical because if students lack the basic vocabulary and facts of the standard, their ability to learn and acquire the necessary skill set for that standard will be significantly impaired. For example, a student who does not know what the term *theme* means cannot possibly understand its purpose in literature.

If students possess this basic knowledge, instruction should move toward what students must Understand, or the big ideas and concepts inherent within the anchor standard. At this stage of learning acquisition, students already possess the core knowledge of the skill, but they struggle with what to do with this knowledge and why it is important to them as readers. Returning to the previous example, students may be able to recite the definition of *theme*, but if they are unable to grasp that narrative elements contribute to the development of the theme, then they will, in turn, fail to develop the skill set necessary to identify themes independently.

After ensuring that students both know and understand key aspects of the anchor standard, educators, only then, should transition toward what students are expected to DO. In the case of theme, possessing a clear definition of theme and equipped with underlying "big ideas" about theme, they are now prepared and confident enough to determine the theme of a given text.

This framework, then, not only allows educators to deconstruct the anchor standards into progressive learning stages, but it also reinforces the understanding that students who struggle cannot be rushed into independently performing applications of anchor standards (e.g., identifying a theme in a given text) without first carefully starting at the foundational level and developing their skill set. Too often, we rush to expect students to demonstrate their knowledge without first providing careful, scaffolded instruction that gradually builds their skills at a pace that is conducive to their learning needs. The KUDOs framework addresses this concern and ensures that students who struggle receive the scaffolding they need to become independent readers and thinkers.

KNOW	UNDERSTAND	DO
Vocabulary	Concepts	Skills
Facts	Generalizations	Applications
What students need to memorize for the standard	What "big idea" students need to take away from the standard	What students need to be able to do independently with the standard
Bloom's Taxonomy: Knowledge	*Bloom's Taxonomy:* Understand	*Bloom's Taxonomy:* Application Analysis Synthesis Evaluation

Targeted Reading Interventions for the Common Core © 2014 by Diana Sisson & Betsy Sisson, Scholastic Teaching Resources

Information at a Glance

Common Core State Standards & Assessment

- Common Core State Standards Web site: **http://www.corestandards.org** (Provides the standards, frequently asked questions, and parent resources)

- Council of Chief State School Officers (CCSSO) Web site: **http://www.ccsso.org/ Resources/Digital_Resources/Common_Core_Implementation_Video_Series. html** (Presents a series of video vignettes to explain the standards in greater depth)

- Smarter Balanced Assessment Consortium Web site: **http://www. smarterbalanced.org** (Contains descriptions of the assessments, practice tests, and released items as well as Common Core State Standards tools and resources for member states belonging to the Smarter Balanced Assessment Consortium)

- Partnership for Assessment of Readiness for College and Careers (PARCC) Assessment Consortium Web site: **http://www.parcconline.org** (Contains descriptions of the assessments, practice tests, sample questions, resources, and updates for member states belonging to the PARCC Assessment Consortium)

Special Interest Groups

- International Reading Association (IRA) Web site: **http://www.reading.org** (Offers books, journals, and resources focused on literacy instruction)

- Teachers of English to Speakers of Other Languages (TESOL) International Organization Web site: **http://www.tesol.org** (Supplies articles, books, tools, and resources for second-language learners)

- National Center for Learning Disabilities (NCLD) Web site: **http://www.ncld. org** (Aligns instructional resources and parent support for students with learning disabilities)

- Council for Exceptional Children (CEC) Web site: **http://www.cec.sped.org** (Recommends best practices for supporting special education students)

Parent Resources

- National Parent Teacher Association (PTA) Web site: **http://www.pta.org/ parents/content.cfm?ItemNumber=2910** (Furnishes brief parent guides by individual grades that explain the Common Core State Standards, delineate what is expected academically at that grade level, highlight what parents can do at home to support their children, and recommend techniques to build a strong home-school relationship; guides are available in both English and Spanish)

- Council of the Great City Schools (CGCS) Web site: **http://www.cgcs.org/Page/328** (Furnishes expanded parent guides by grade level that explain what is expected of students academically with the Common Core State Standards—with both literature and informational text—and place the grade levels in context by illustrating expectations from the previous grade as well as the upcoming grade; also suggests ways parents can help their children learn outside of school; guides are available in both English and Spanish)

Instruction Resources

- Achieve the Core Web site: **http://www.achievethecore.org** (Offers a range of supports, including lesson plans, student writing samples, assessment questions, curricular tools, techniques for supporting all students, and professional development)

- Association for Supervision and Curriculum Development (ASCD) Web site: **http://educore.ascd.org** (Makes available a collection of tools, strategies, videos, and resources specifically designed for implementing Common Core State Standards)

Student Reading Materials

(*Literature, Informational Text, Drama, and Poetry*)

- Clarkness.com: **http://www.clarkness.com/index.htm** (Delivers hundreds of free stories and e-books for the beginning reader)

- Dr. Young's Reading Room (Texas A & M University): **http://www.thebestclass.org/rtscripts.html** (Furnishes Readers Theater scripts)

- Giggle Poetry: **http://www.gigglepoetry.com/** (Provides a range of fun poems)

- Harvard Classics: **http://www.bartleby.com/17/1/** (Makes available over 80 of Aesop's fables)

- Internet4Classrooms: **http://www.internet4classrooms.com/grade_level_help.htm** (Grants access to grade-level skill builders and Common Core-aligned stories, activities, and resources)

- NEWSELA: **http://www.newsela.com** (Presents current events texts at a range of grade levels and lexiles—educators can select a text and then raise or lower the grade level/lexile based on the needs of their students; also aligned to Common Core State Standards.)

- Read Me a Story, Ink: **http://www.readmeastoryink.com/index.php** (Supplies over 1,000 read-aloud short stories and book recommendations with a search feature by story category and grade)

Glossary of Terms

Below is a glossary of key vocabulary terms related to the anchor standards. Definitions have been simplified for classroom instructional use.

Alliteration: Repetition of initial consonant sounds; example: *Peter Piper picked a peck of pickled peppers.*

Allusion: A reference to a person, place, or event (real or fictionalized)

Analogy: A comparison of two things upon which comparisons may be made

Author: The person who wrote the text

Central message: Synonymous with theme or lesson; see "Theme"

Character: The person or animal in a story; characters can be described through both direct (what the author actually says) and indirect characterization (what the characters do, say, think, feel or look like).

Connotative meanings: Words associated with a term; example: *The terms* gentleman, dude, *and* guy *are connotative words associated with* man.

Dialogue: Conversation between two or more characters

Digital text: Electronic version of a printed text

Drama: A serious narrative; a play

Drawing conclusions: The synthesis of facts and the reader's prior knowledge to infer relationships, judge occurrences, and predict events

Explicit: Clearly stated

Event: A specific thing that happens in the story; individual events help propel the story forward; this can best be explained by answering the following questions: What happened first? Then what happened? What happened next? How did the story end?

Evidence: Details that prove conclusion or judgment

Fable: A fictionalized story that contains animals as characters and attempts to teach a moral, or lesson, to the reader; example: *"The Lion and the Mouse" from Aesop's fables*

Fantasy story: A fictionalized story that contains magic or supernatural characteristics; example: *the Harry Potter series by J. K. Rowling*

Fiction: A made-up text created by an author

Figurative language: A description of something made through comparisons; typically requires the reader to use his or her imagination; examples: *simile, metaphor, onomatopoeia, personification, alliteration, hyperbole*

Flashback: A part of a narrative that occurs when the author suddenly interrupts the flow of the story to jump back to earlier events; example: *a story begins when a person is quite old, but then jumps backward in time to when he or she was a child.*

Folktale: A fictionalized story that has been orally passed down through generations of a people

Historical novel: A fictionalized story set in an actual period of history; example: The Midwife's Apprentice *by Karen Cushman (1995)*

Hyperbole: An exaggeration so great as not to be believed; example: *The students have a mountain of homework.*

Illustration: A picture in a text

Illustrator: A person who creates pictures for a text

Inference: A conclusion based on reasoning from evidence

Irony: The contrast between what is expected and what actually exists or happens; example: *It would be ironic if a champion swimmer hated to swim.*

Lesson: Synonymous with central message or theme; see "Theme"

Media: Means of communication; examples: *printed text, electronic text, audio recording, videotaped production*

Metaphor: A comparison of unlike things without using the words *like* or *as*; example: *She is a rose.*

Meter: The measured arrangement of words in poetry

Moral: Synonymous with theme or lesson; see "Theme"

Multimedia: The combined use of several media forms

Mythology: Fictionalized stories from ancient times that attempt to explain the natural world; example: *the Greek myth of Demeter and the changing seasons*

Narrator: The person who tells the story

Opinion: A belief about something

Onomatopoeia: A word that describes or imitates a sound from nature; example: *A snake hisses*.

Personification: An animal or object that takes on human characteristics; example: *The wind whistled in the trees*.

Poem: A text meant to convey ideas and emotions, typically using rhyme, rhythm, and meter

Poetry: A text containing qualities found in poems

Point of view: How an author decides to tell a story; example: *Who is telling the story? If you see the words "I," "me," or "we," then it's a first-person point of view; if you see the words "you" or "your," then it's a second-person point of view; if you see the words "he," "she," or "they," then it's a third-person point of view*.

Plot: The main events of a story; a well-developed plot has a cause-and-effect pattern—one event naturally leads to another

Problem: An obstacle that prevents a character from reaching his or her goal; stories must have problems—without the characters experiencing a problem, the story lacks interest.

Prose: A piece of text that uses everyday written language—in contrast to poetry, which utilizes a metrical structure; prose encompasses literature, informational text, and drama.

Purpose: The reason an author writes something

Resolution: A solution to the problem in a story

Rhyme: A regular matching of sounds, typically at the end of words; example: *dog and frog*

Rhythm: A pattern of recurring sounds

Sarcasm: The use of words to mean the opposite of what is actually said

Satire: A fictionalized text that attempts to highlight human weakness or vice to ridicule it

Scene: The division in a play that encompasses a single unit of development within the plot of the story

Section: A major part of a text

Setting: The time and place in which story events happen; the setting can be determined through looking at the styles of buildings, transportation, language, and clothing described in the text.

Simile: A comparison of unlike things using the words *like* or *as*; example: *She is as pretty as a rose*.

Soliloquy: A dramatic discourse in which a character talks to himself or herself and reveals his or her thoughts

Solution: How the problem in the plot is resolved; the problem in the story must be resolved in some way—the reader may not like the solution, but a solution of some nature must exist.

Sonnet: A poem comprised of 14 lines and typically expressing one central theme or idea

Stanza: A division of a poem with at least two lines, usually characterized by a common meter and rhyme

Summarize: To group main points together to form a short, clear understanding of a text; to summarize effectively, distinguish between ideas that the author deems important and those that are interesting but secondary; also differentiate between main ideas (something repeated throughout the text) and details (something found only once or twice in the text).

Supporting details: The individual parts of the whole text that contribute to the main idea or central idea

Technical meanings: Specialized vocabulary in a given field

Text: Written or printed words

Text structure: How information is organized; (1) main idea text structure presents important information on a specific topic and gives characteristics about that topic; (2) sequence of events text structure presents a number of ideas or events in a succession; (3) compare/contrast text structure presents likenesses and differences between two objects or ideas; (4) cause/effect text structure presents ideas so that reasons and consequences can be identified.

Textual evidence: Details from a text that support the conclusion drawn by the reader

Theme: A lesson a story teaches

Tone: The atmosphere that the writer creates in his story; example: *Ask yourself how the story makes you feel? Joyful? Sad? Hopeful?*

Topic: The subject of a text

Traditional literature: Literature that has existed in a culture for a long period of time; see "Folktale"

Verse: A single line of poetry

 Targeted Reading Interventions for the Common Core © 2014 by Diana Sisson & Betsy Sisson, Scholastic Teaching Resources

References

Afflerbach, P., & Cho, B. (2009). Identifying and describing constructively responsive comprehension strategies in new and traditional forms of reading. In S. E. Israel & G. G. Duffy (Eds.), *Handbook of research on reading comprehension*. New York: Routledge.

Akhondi, M., Malayeri, F. A., & Samad, A. A. (2011). How to teach expository text structure to facilitate reading comprehension. *The Reading Teacher, 64*(5), 368–372. doi: 10.1598/RT.64.5.9

Allbery, D. (2010). Bridging fact and story: Using historical fiction in middle school social studies. In S. Szabo, T. Morrison, L. Martin, M. Boggs, I. Raine (Eds.), *Building literacy communities: The thirty-second yearbook: A doubled peer reviewed publication of the Association of Literacy Educators and Researchers*. Louisville, KY: Association of Literacy Educators and Researchers.

Alvermann, D. E., Swafford, J., & Montero, M. K. (2004). *Content area literacy instruction for the elementary grades*. Boston: Allyn & Bacon.

Artley, A. S. (1943). Teaching word-meaning through context. *The Elementary English Review, 20*(2), 68–74.

Ash, G. E. (2005). What did Abigail mean? *Educational Leadership, 63*(2), 36–41.

August, D., Carlo, M., Dressler, C., & Snow, C. (2005). The critical role of vocabulary development for English language learners. *Learning Disabilities Research and Practice, 20*(1), 50–57. doi: 10.1111/j.1540-5826.2005.00120.x

Bakken, J. P., & Whedon, C. K. (2002). Teaching text structure to improve reading comprehension. *Intervention in school and clinic, 37*(4), 229–233. doi: 10.1177/105345120203700406

Barnes, A. C., & Harlacher, J. E. (2008). Clearing the confusion: Response-to-Intervention as a set of principles. *Education and Treatment of Children, 31*, 417–431.

Basaraba, D., Yovanoff, P., Alonzo, J., & Tindal, G. (2013). Examining the structure of reading comprehension: Do literal, inferential, and evaluative comprehension truly exist? *Reading & Writing, 26*, 349–379. doi:10.1007/s11145-012-9372-9

Baumann, J. F. (2005). Vocabulary-comprehension relationships. In B. Maloch, J. V. Hoffman, D. L. Schallert, C. M. Fairbanks, & J. Worthy (Eds.), *Fifty-fourth yearbook of the National Reading Conference* (pp. 117–131). Oak Creek, WI: National Reading Conference.

Baumann, J. F., Kame'enui, E. J., & Ash, G. E. (2003). Research on vocabulary instruction: Voltaire redux. In J. Flood, D. Lapp, J. R. Squire, & J. M. Jensen (Eds.), *Handbook of research on teaching the English language arts* (2nd ed.). (pp. 752–785). Mahwah, NJ: Lawrence Erlbaum Associates.

Biancarosa, G. (2012). Adolescent literacy: More than remediation. *Educational Leadership, 69*(6), 22–27.

Blachowicz, C., & Ogle, D. (2008). *Reading comprehension: Strategies for independent learners*. New York: The Guilford Press.

Bloom, B. S. (Ed.). (1956). *Taxonomy of educational objectives: Book 1 cognitive domain*. White Plains, NY: Longman.

Boling, C. J., & Evans, W. H. (2008). Reading success in the secondary classroom. *Preventing school failure: Alternative education for children and youth, 52*(2), 59–66. doi:10.3200/PSFL.52.2.59-66

Brabham, E. G., & Villaume, S. K. (2002). Leveled text: The good news and the bad news. *The Reading Teacher, 55*(5), 438–441.

Bråten, I., Britt, M. A., Strømsø, H. I., & Rouet, J. (2011). The role of epistemic beliefs in the comprehension of multiple expository texts: Toward an integrated model. *Educational Psychologies, 46*(1), 48–70. doi: 10.1080/00461520.2011.538647

Bus, A. G., & Neuman, S. B. (2009). *Multimedia and literacy development: Improving achievement for young learners*. New York: Taylor & Francis.

Cain, K. (2009). Making sense of text: Skills that support text comprehension and its development. *Perspectives on Language and Literacy, 35*(2), 11–14.

Calkins, L. (1994). *The art of teaching writing*. Portsmouth, NH: Heinemann.

Carlisle, J. F. (2007). Fostering morphological processing, vocabulary development, and reading comprehension. In R. K. Wagner, A. E. Muse, & K. R. Tannenbaum (Eds.), *Vocabulary acquisition: Implications for reading comprehension*. New York: The Guilford Press.

Chauvin, R., & Molina, C. (2012). Secondary content-area literacy: Time for crisis or opportunity for reform? Retrieved from http://txcc.sedl.org/resources/briefs/number_12/index.php

Coiro, J. (2003a). Reading comprehension on the Internet: Expanding our understanding of reading comprehension to encompass new literacies. *The Reading Teacher, 56*(5), 458–464.

Coiro, J. (2003b). Rethinking comprehension strategies to better prepare students for critically evaluating content on the Internet. *The NERA Journal, 39*(2), 29–34.

Coiro, J. (2007). *Exploring changes to reading comprehension on the Internet: Paradoxes and possibilities for diverse adolescent readers*. (Doctoral dissertation, University of Connecticut, 2007). Retrieved from http://gradworks.umi.com/32/70/3270969.html

Coiro, J., Knobel, M., Lankshear, C., & Leu, D. J. (Ed.). (2008). *Handbook of research on new literacies*. New York: Taylor & Francis.

Colby, S. A., & Lyon, A. F. (2004). Heightening awareness about the importance of using multicultural literature. *Multicultural Education, 11*(3), 24–28.

Coleman, D. (2011). David Coleman: Common Core: Summer 2011. [YouTube] DC Public Schools. Podcast retrieved from www.youtube.com/watch?v=aTCiQVCpdQc

Davis, F. B. (1944). Fundamental factors of comprehension of reading. *Psychometrika, 9*, 185–197.

Deane, P., Sheehan, K. M., Sabatini, J., Futagi, Y., & Kostin, I. (2006). Differences in text structure and its implications for assessment of struggling readers. *Scientific Studies of Reading, 10*(3), 257–275. doi: 10.1207/s1532799xssr1003_4

Duke, N. K., Caughlan, S., Juzwik, M. M., & Martin, N. M. (2012). Teaching genre with purpose. *Educational Leadership, 69*(6), 34–39.

Duke, N. K., & Pearson, P. D. (2002). Effective practices for developing reading comprehension. In A. E. Farstrup & S. J. Samuels (Eds.), *What research has to say about reading comprehension.* Newark, DE: International Reading Association.

Duke, N. K., & Roberts, K. M. (2010). The genre-specific nature of reading comprehension. In D. Wyse, R. Andrews, & J. Hoffman (Eds.), *The Routledge international handbook of English, language and literacy teaching* (pp. 74–86). London: Routledge.

Dymock, S. (2005). Teaching expository text structure awareness. *The Reading Teacher, 59*(2), 177–181. doi: 10.1598/RT.59.2.7

Dymock, S. (2007). Comprehension strategy instruction: Teaching narrative text structure awareness. *The Reading Teacher, 61*(2), 161–167. doi: 10.1598/RT.61.2.6

Ebe, A. E. (2010). Culturally relevant texts and reading assessment for English language learners. *Reading Horizons, 50*(3), 193–210.

Fisher, D., & Frey, N. (2012). Close reading in elementary schools. *The Reading Teacher, 66*(3), 179–188. doi: 10.1002/TRTR.01117

Fisher, D., Frey, N., & Lapp, D. (2012). *Text complexity: Raising rigor in reading.* Newark, DE: International Reading Association.

Fleischman, S. (1986). *The whipping boy.* New York: Greenwillow.

Freebody, P., & Luke, A. (1990). "Literacies" programs: Debates and demands in cultural context. *Prospect, 5*(5) 7–16.

Fuchs, D., Fuchs, L. S., & Vaughn, S. (2008). *Response to intervention: A framework for reading educators.* Newark, DE: International Reading Association.

Fukkink, R. J., & de Glopper, J. (1998). Effects of instruction in deriving word meaning from context: A meta-analysis. *Review of Educational Research, 68*(4), 450–469. doi: 10.3102/00346543068004450

Fulton, L., & Poeltler, E. (2013). Developing a scientific argument. *Science & Children, 59*(9), 30–35.

Gambrell, L. B., Malloy, J. A., & Mazzoni, S. A. (2011). Evidence-based best practices in comprehensive literacy instruction. In L. M. Morrow & M. B. Gambrell (Eds.), *Best practices in literacy instruction* (pp. 11–36). New York: The Guilford Press.

Gewertz, C. (2013, October 9). Global study identifies promising practices in top-scoring nations. *Education Week,* p. 9. Retrieved from www.eduweek.org/ew/articles/2013

Gill, S. R. (2008). The comprehension matrix: A tool for designing comprehension instruction. *The Reading Teacher, 62*(2), 106–113. doi: 10.1598/RT.62.2.2

Goetz, S., & Walker, B. J. (2004). At-risk readers can construct complex meanings: Technology can help. *The Reading Teacher, 57*(8), 778–780.

Gomez-Zwiep, S., & Harris, D. (2010). Supporting ideas with evidence. *Science & Children, 48*(1), 76–79.

Goodman, K. S. (1965). A linguistic study of cues and miscues in reading. *Elementary English, 42*, 639–643.

Graves, M. F., & Watts-Taffe, S. M. (2002). The place of word consciousness in a research-based vocabulary program. In A. E. Farstrup & S. J. Samuels, (Eds.), *What research has to say about reading instruction.* Newark, DE: International Reading Association.

Greenwood, C. R., Kamps, D., Terry, B., & Linebarger, D. (2007). Primary intervention: A means of preventing special education? In C. Haager, J. Klingner, & S. Vaughn, (Eds.), *Validated Reading Practices for Three Tiers of Intervention* (pp. 73–106). New York: Brookes.

Griffith, P. L., & Ruan, J. (2005). What is metacognition and what should be its role in literacy instruction? In S. E. Israel, C. C. Block, K. L. Bauserman, & K. Kinnucan-Welsch, (Eds.), *Metacognition in literacy learning: Theory, assessment, instruction, and professional development.* Mahwah: NJ: Lawrence Erlbaum Associates.

Harvey, S., & Goudvis, A. (2000). *Strategies that work: Teaching comprehension for understanding and engagement.* Portland, ME: Stenhouse.

Heacox, D. (2009). *Making differentiation a habit.* Minneapolis, MN: Free Spirit Publishing Inc.

Herber, H. L. (1970). *Teaching reading in the content areas.* Englewood Cliffs, NJ: Prentice Hall.

Herman, D. (2009). *Basic elements of narrative.* Malden, MA: John Wiley & Sons.

Hirsch, Jr., E. D. (2003, Spring). Reading comprehension requires knowledge—of words and the world: Scientific insights into the fourth-grade slump and the nation's stagnant comprehension scores. *American Educator,* 10–22, 28–29, 44.

Hynd, C. R. (1999). Teaching students to think critically using multiple texts in history. *Journal of Adolescent & Adult Literacy,* 428–436.

Johnson, J. C. (2005). What makes a "good" reader? Asking students to define "good" readers. *The Reading Teacher, 58*(8), 766–770. doi: 10.1598/RT.58.8.6

Juel, C., & Deffes, R. (2004). Making words stick. *Educational Leadership, 61*(6), 30–34.

Kamil, M. L., & Hiebert, E. H. (2005). Teaching and learning vocabulary: Perspectives and persistent issues. In M. L. Kamil and E. H. Hiebert (Eds.), *Teaching and learning vocabulary* (pp. 1–26). Mahway, NJ: Lawrence Erlbaum.

Keene, E. O., & Zimmermann, S. (1997). *Mosaic of thought*. Portsmouth, NH: Heinemann.

Kellner, D. (2001). New technologies/new literacies: Reconstructing education for the new millennium. *International Journal of Technology and Design Education, 11*(1), 67–81.

Kieffer, M. J., & Lesaux, N. K. (2007). Breaking down words to build meanings: Morphology, vocabulary and reading comprehension in the urban classroom. *The Reading Teacher, 61*(2), 134–144. doi: 10.1598/RT.61.2.3

Kincade, K. M., & Pruitt, N. E. (1996). Using multicultural literature as an ally to elementary social studies texts. *Literacy Research and Instruction, 36*(1), 18–32.

Kintsch, W., & Rawson, K. A. (2005). Comprehension. In M. J. Snowling & C. Hulme (Eds.), *The science of reading: A handbook* (pp. 209–226). Malden, MA: Blackwell.

Kruse, M. (2001). Escaping ethnic encapsulation: The role of multicultural children's literature. *Delta Kappa Gamma Bulletin, 67*(2), 26–32.

Kuzminski, P. (2002). The effective use of literature in preparing children for a global society. *Delta Kappa Gamma Bulletin, 69*(1), 19–22.

Landt, S. M. (2006). Multicultural literature and young adolescents: A kaleidoscope of opportunity. *Journal of Adolescent & Adult Literacy, 49*(8), 690–697.

Larson, A. A., Britt, M. A., & Kurby, C. A. (2009). Improving students' evaluation of informal arguments. *The Journal of Experimental Education, 77*(4), 339–366.

Lervåg, A., & Aukrust, V. G. (2009). Vocabulary knowledge is a critical determinant of the difference in reading comprehension growth between first and second language learners. *The Journal of Child Psychology and Psychiatry, 51*(5), 612–620. doi: 10.1111/j.1469-7610.2009.02185.x

Leu, D. J., Jr. (2000). Our children's future: Changing the focus of literacy and literacy instruction. *The Reading Teacher, 53*(5), 424–429.

Louie, B. Y. (2011). Guiding principles for teaching multicultural literature. *The Reading Teacher, 59*(5), 438–448. doi: 10.1598/RT.59.5.3

Lubliner, S., & Smetana, L. (2005). The effects of comprehensive vocabulary instruction on Title I students' metacognitive word-learning skills and reading comprehension. *Journal of Literacy Research, 37*, 163–200.

Lyon, G. R. (1998). Overview of reading and literacy research. In S. Patton & M. Holmes (Eds.), *The keys to literacy*. Washington, DC: Council for Basic Education.

Massey, D. D., & Heafner, T. L. (2004). Promoting reading comprehension in social studies. *Journal of Adolescent & Adult Literacy, 48*(1), 26–40. doi: 10.1598/JAAL.48.1.3

McGregor, T. (2007). *Comprehension connections: Bridges to strategic reading*. Portsmouth, NH: Heinemann.

Mellard, D. F., & Johnson, E. (2008). *RTI: A practitioner's guide to implementing response to intervention*. Thousand Oaks, CA: A Joint Publication of Corwin Press.

Mesmer, H. A., Cunningham, J. W., & Hiebert, E. H. (2012). Toward a theoretical model of text complexity for the early grades: Learning from the past, anticipating the future. *Reading Research Quarterly, 47*(3), 235–258. doi: 10.1002/rrq.019

Meyer, B. J. F. (1987). Following the author's top-level organization: An important skill for reading comprehension. In R. J. Tierney, P. L. Anders, & J. N. Mitchell (Eds.), *Understanding readers' understanding: Theory and practice*, (pp. 59–76). Hillsdale, NJ: Erlbaum.

Meyer, B. J. F., & Ray, M. N. (2011). Structure strategy interventions: Increasing reading comprehension of expository text. *International Electronic Journal of Elementary Education, 4*(1), 127–152.

Molden, K. (2007). Critical literacy, the right answer for the reading classroom: Strategies to move beyond comprehension for reading comprehension. *Reading Improvement, 44*(1), 50–56.

Moss, B. (2011). Making a case and a place for effective content area literacy instruction in the elementary grades. *The Reading Teacher, 59*(1), 46–55. doi: 10.1598

Nagy, W. E., & Anderson, R. C. (1987). Learning word meanings from context during normal reading. *American Educational Research Journal, 24*(2), 237–270. doi: 10.3102/00028312024002237

Nation, K. (2005). Children's reading comprehension difficulties. In M. J. Snowling & C. Hulme (Eds.), *The science of reading: A handbook* (pp. 248–265). Malden, MA: Blackwell.

National Governors Association Center for Best Practices & Council of Chief State School Officers. (2010). *Common Core State Standards for English language arts and literacy in history/social studies, science, and technical subjects*. Washington, DC: Authors.

National Institute of Child Health and Student Development, Report of the National Reading Panel, *Teaching children to read: An evidence-based assessment of scientific research literature on reading and its implications for reading instruction*. (2000). (NIH Publication No. 00-4769). Washington, DC: U.S. Government Printing Office.

Neuman, S. B., & Roskos, K. (2012). How children become more knowledgeable through text. *The Reading Teacher, 66*(3), 207–210. doi: 10.1002/TRTR.01118

Nussbaum, E. M. (2008). Collaborative discourse, argumentation, and learning: Preface and literature review. *Contemporary Educational Psychology, 33*(3), 345–359.

Ogle, D., & Blachowicz, C. L. Z. (2002). Beyond literature circles: Helping students comprehend information texts. In C. C. Block & M. Pressley (Eds.), *Comprehension instruction: Research-based best practices,* (pp. 259–274). New York: The Guilford Press.

Pardo, L. S. (2004). What every teacher needs to know about comprehension. *The Reading Teacher, 58*(3), 272–280. doi: 10.1598/RT.58.3.5

Paul, R., & Elder, L. (2003). Critical thinking . . . and the art of close reading (Part 1). *Journal of Developmental Education, 27*(2), 36–37, 39.

Perfetti, C. A., Marron, M. A., & Foltz, P. W. (1996). Sources of comprehension failure: Theoretical perspectives and case studies. In C. Cornoldi & J. Oakhill (Eds.), *Reading comprehension difficulties: Processes and intervention* (pp. 137–165). Mahwah, NJ: Lawrence Erlbaum.

Ranker, J. (2011). Learning nonfiction in an ESL class: The interaction of situated practice and teacher scaffolding in a genre study. *The Reading Teacher, 62*(7), 580–589. doi: 10.1598/RT.62.7.4

Richek, M. (2005). Words are wonderful: Interactive, time-efficient strategies to teach meaning vocabulary. *The Reading Teacher, 58*(5), 414–423.

Ross, E. P. (1981). Checking the source: An essential component of critical reading. *Journal of Reading, 24*(4), 311–315.

Rouet, J., Lowe, R., Schnotz, W. (Eds.), (2008). *Understanding multimedia documents.* New York: Springer.

Rowe, J. P., McQuiggan, S. W., & Lester, J. C. (2007). *Narrative presence in intelligent learning environments.* Working Notes of the 2007 AAAI Fall Symposium on Intelligent Narrative Technologies, 126–133.

Santoro, L. E., Chard, D. J., Howard, L., & Baker, S. K. (2008). Making the very most of classroom read alouds to promote comprehension and vocabulary. *The Reading Teacher, 61*(5), 396–408.

Sencibaugh, J. M. (2005). *Meta-analysis of reading comprehension interventions for students with learning disabilities: Strategies and implications.* Retrieved at ERIC database. (ED493483)

Shanahan, T., Fisher, D., & Frey, N. (2012). The challenge of challenging text. *Educational Leadership, 69*(6), 58–63.

Simpson, P. (1993). *Language, ideology and point of view.* New York: Routledge.

Sinatra, R. C. (2000). Teaching learners to think, read, and write more effectively in content subjects. *The Clearing House, 73*(5), 266–273. doi: 10.1080/00098650009600967

Sisson, D., & Sisson, B. (2014). *Close reading in elementary school: Bringing readers and texts together.* New York: Taylor & Francis.

Smith, C. B. (1994). *Helping children understand literary genres.* Bloomington, IN: ERIC Clearinghouse on Reading, English, and Communication. (Document # ED366985)

Smith, N. B. (1974). *The classroom teacher's responsibility to the disabled reader.* Paper presented at the International Reading Association World Congress on Reading, Vienna,

Austria. Abstract retrieved from http://files.eric.ed.gov/fulltext/ED095496.pdf

Snow, C. E. (2002). *Reading for understanding: Toward a R&D program in reading comprehension.* Santa Monica, CA: RAND.

Stahl, S., & Nagy, W. (2006). *Teaching word meanings.* Mahwah, NJ: Lawrence Erlbaum.

Sternberg, R. J. (1987). Most vocabulary is learned from context. In M. G. McKeown & M. E. Curtis (Eds.), *The nature of vocabulary acquisition,* (pp. 89–105). Hillsdale, NJ: Lawrence Erlbaum.

Stetter, M. E., & Hughes, M. T. (2010). Using story grammar to assist students with learning disabilities and reading difficulties improve their comprehension. *Education and Treatment of Children, 33*(1), 115–151. doi: 10.1353/etc.0.0087

Stobaugh, R. (2013). *How to teach students to evaluate information: A key Common Core skill.* Larchmont, NY: Eye on Education.

Taylor, L. K., Abler, S. R., & Walker, D. W. (2002). The comparative effects of a modified self-questioning strategy and story mapping on the reading comprehension of elementary students with learning disabilities. *Journal of Behavioral Education, 11*(2), 69–87.

Taylor, S. V. (2000). Multicultural is who we are: Literature as a reflection of ourselves. *Teaching Exceptional Children, 32*(3), 24–29.

Tovani, C. (2004). *Do I really have to teach reading? Content comprehension, Grades 6–12.* Portland, ME: Stenhouse Publishers.

van Peer, W., & Chatman, S. (Eds.), (2001). *New perspectives on narrative perspective.* Albany, NY: State University of New York Press.

Voss, J. F., & Wiley, J. (2000). A case study of developing historical understanding via instruction. In P. N. Stearns, P. Seixas, & S. Wineburg (Eds.), *Knowing, teaching, and learning history: National and international perspectives* (pp. 375–389). New York: New York University Press.

Vygotsky, L. S. (1962). *Thought and language.* (E. Hanfmann & G. Vakar, Eds. & Trans.). Cambridge, MA: MIT. (Original work published 1934)

Vygotsky, L. S. (1978). *Mind in society: The development of higher psychological processes.* Cambridge, MA: Harvard University Press.

Warschauer, M. (2007). The paradoxical future of digital learning. *Learning Inquiry, 1*(1), 41–49.

White, C. E. & Kim, J. S. (2009). *Putting the pieces of the puzzle together: How systematic vocabulary instruction and expanded learning time can address the literacy gap.* Washington, DC.: Center for American Progress.

Zimmermann, S., & Hutchins C. (2003). *7 keys to comprehension.* New York: Three Rivers Press.